From Discipline to Development
Rethinking Student Conduct in Higher Education

by Michael Dannells

ASHE-ERIC Higher Education Report Volume 25, Number 2

Prepared by

Clearinghouse on Higher Education
The George Washington University

In cooperation with

Association for the Study
of Higher Education

Published by

Graduate School of Education and Human Development
The George Washington University

Jonathan D. Fife, Series Editor

Cite as
Dannells, Michael. 1997. *From Discipline to Development: Rethinking Student Conduct in Higher Education*. ASHE-ERIC Higher Education Report Volume 25, No. 2. Washington, D.C. The George Washington University, Graduate School of Education and Human Development.

Library of Congress Catalog Card Number 97-70270
ISSN 0884-0040
ISBN 1-878380-74-5

Managing Editor: Lynne J. Scott
Manuscript Editor: Sandra Selva
Cover Design by Michael David Brown, Inc. The Red Door Gallery, Rockport, ME

The ERIC Clearinghouse on Higher Education invites individuals to submit proposals for writing monographs for the *ASHE-ERIC Higher Education Report* series. Proposals must include:
1. A detailed manuscript proposal of not more than five pages.
2. A chapter-by-chapter outline.
3. A 75-word summary to be used by several review committees for the initial screening and rating of each proposal.
4. A vita and a writing sample.

ERIC Clearinghouse on Higher Education
Graduate School of Education and Human Development
The George Washington University
One Dupont Circle, Suite 630
Washington, DC 20036-1183

> *The mission of the ERIC system is to improve American education by increasing and facilitating the use of educational research and information on practice in the activities of learning, teaching, educational decision making, and research, wherever and whenever these activities take place.*

This publication was prepared partially with funding from the Office of Education Research and Improvement, U.S. Department of Education, under contract no. ED RR-93-002008. The opinions expressed in this report do not necessarily reflect the positions or policies of OERI or the Department.

EXECUTIVE SUMMARY

Student discipline has been a point of concern and contention for most of the history of higher education in the United States; today is no exception. Perhaps no other single subject so dramatically reflects our attitudes about students and how we define our duty and our relationship with them. From the earliest dissatisfactions with pious and moralistic paternalism in the colonial colleges, to recent controversies over hate speech versus First Amendment rights, student behavior and institutional responses have vexed faculty and administrators with a set of issues both fundamental and timely. Why do we concern ourselves with student behavior at all? What should be the "reach" of the institutions of higher education? What standards of behavior should colleges expect? How are those standards best communicated? By what processes should misconduct be adjudicated? If standards are broken, how should institutions respond? What is our overreaching purpose in student discipline? How do we know when it is met? Who should be responsible for it?

Student discipline comprises a set of complex and interrelated issues that deserve careful examination and reasonable recommendations. This report provides both, with an eye toward new trends in responding to and preventing student misconduct, and to programs that avoid unduly legalistic processes, while enhancing student development in the continuation of the institutional mission.

What role should colleges and universities play in student discipline?

Once student discipline was a central part of the college mission; today, it has moved to the periphery of most campus agendas. Since the demise of *in loco parentis*, most campuses have been left without a guiding reason for engaging in student discipline, and most faculty are, at best, only marginally involved in day-to-day matters of student conduct. Even campus administrators are ambivalent about their overall duty for student behavior.

Urgent present-day concerns about such behavioral problems as crime on campus, hate speech, date/acquaintance rape, alcohol (and other substance) abuse, and academic dishonesty, coupled with demands for greater supervision of students, the increasing litigiousness of a civil-liberty minded populace, as well as an increase in older, more consumer-oriented students, have left campus leaders understandably wary, while searching for new ways to fashion policy in this area. As a legacy of the student rights movement of the 1960s and 1970s, and the accompanying judicial scrutiny of disciplinary decisions, today's codes of conduct tend to be heavy on process and light on real guidance for the student. It is time for colleges and universities to rethink their purposes for engaging in student discipline and fashion rules and processes that follow logically. Hoekema (1994) has proposed a useful, and thoughtful analytic framework and conceptual model for thinking about codes of conduct, based on three overarching moral/ethical principles: preventing harm, upholding freedom, and fostering community. Many campuses could benefit from a close consideration of this approach.

Where should institutions begin in reconsidering student discipline, and who should be involved?
Colleges and universities are urged to reconsider their approaches to student discipline by attempting to integrate the academic and nonacademic worlds of students through a broad-based, unified approach that demonstrates and reinforces the importance and integrity of institutional values. They should begin this process by reviewing and clarifying institutional values as they are already articulated in mission statements, codes of conduct, and academic integrity policies. Given the current high level of concern about student cheating, it may be the best and safest place to begin; few would argue with academia's hand in this domain. Faculty, administrative and student affairs staff, and students should all be involved in a collaborative effort. Honor codes are in resurgence and should be carefully considered. There is a growing body of research that supports their efficacy, and while they are certainly not a panacea, the very process of considering an honor code should stimulate the kind of value-focused dialogue necessary for the campus to become a more moral community. Another good place to begin promoting such community building is in the curriculum. Astin (1995) recently proposed a "citizenship curriculum," which could foster the basic democratic values reinforcing and undergirding the campus disciplinary program. Many colleges and universities are instituting interdisciplinary courses to meet general education needs and to challenge the values

of a materialistic, philosophic student body. Shouldn't there be room for a course, perhaps even a required course, that directly addresses student rights and responsibilities in the campus community?

What more do we need to learn about student discipline?

Although institutions of higher education in the United States have been engaged in the practice of student discipline for more than 300 years, we know surprisingly little about the effectiveness of our efforts. Research in student discipline should be conducted in three areas. First, institutional research should be done on existing disciplinary programs to determine their present effectiveness. Like any other student development program, these efforts should be periodically and systematically evaluated to ensure they are meeting their goals. The practice of disciplinary counseling should be of particular interest. It is a commonly employed response to student misbehavior, yet it has been questioned on the basis of ethics and efficacy. Second, student behavior, and how it is affected by the predominant student culture, its various subcultures, and how they compare to the faculty culture, should be studied. Conventional survey techniques, as well as qualitative methods, especially ethnographic, should be used to conduct "culture audits." Third, student development theories need to be operationalized and tested in the disciplinary context. If traditional quantitative methods do not seem to convey the richness of data needed by disciplinary practitioners, then qualitative methods should be encouraged. The case study method is a useful way of linking developmental theory to disciplinary practice, yet it is rare in the student personnel literature.

In what ways must campuses change to foster the development of disciplined students?

Colleges and universities and their students would benefit by thinking about student discipline in less adversarial and more developmental ways. Many disputes that now fill campus judicial systems might be better resolved through mediation. If disciplinary counseling is too problematic in the way we currently think about our disciplinary/judicial systems, perhaps we need to reframe our approach to include such methods as "caring confrontation," wherein the student's behavior is critically examined in a supportive relationship, and the central goal of the process is to see what can be learned from the situation, but not so much the determination of guilt and the application of punishment.

Student affairs leaders, and in particular the chief student affairs officer (CSAO) on campus, must actively and positively embrace their responsibility to encourage the building of moral/ethical communities on campus. The best student discipline program is the preventative type that creates a campus environment of caring and compassion, and one that deters hateful and destructive behavior by virtue of commitment to the community. One of the most effective ways to achieve the building of such a commitment is through service learning. College students, especially young college students, who have had the opportunity to learn about the needs of others through service to them, are far less likely to engage in the kinds of selfish and immature behaviors that account for the bulk of the disciplinary caseloads at most institutions. CSAOs, with their expertise in experiential learning, and with the opportunity to promote such programs through a myriad of student services, are in a unique position to contribute to the curriculum and promote the development of the whole student.

The importance of building more caring and collaborative communities of learning on our campuses has been a consistent theme in the literature on higher education for almost a decade. Student discipline can play a vital part, but first, institutions must clarify their values, and then campus leaders—including both academic affairs and student affairs—must take responsibility for developing disciplinary programs which are fair, humane, and uphold those values for the betterment of the individual student and for the community as a whole.

CONTENTS

FOREWORD

Historically, student discipline has been looked upon as an institutional responsibility. The concept of institutions acting en loco parentis had its origin based on the authority of the king for his subjects and on the legality that the colonial colleges were in fact acting "in place of the parent" since the colleges' students of colonial time were often only 13 or 14 years old. As the country expanded in the early and mid 1800s, small, religious-oriented colleges were established and used student discipline as their way to reinforce moral teachings of their religious beliefs. In the 1950s and 1960s, with the explosion of public higher education institutions, student discipline was seen as a necessary condition to maintain an orderly institution and to provide some pre-dictability for day to day interactions.

Since the early 1970s, three conditions have occurred that now makes it appropriate to revisit the purpose of student discipline. The first major change was the lowering of the age of majority from 21 to 18. This dramatically changed the relationship of institution to the student from that of caretaker of minors to a contractual relationship with adults. The second change is that a large percentage of this adult population moved from a population of 18 to 21 year old, full-time students to part-time students in their late twenties and early thirties. The third change is the dramatic increase in students from different cultures and different races. More and more, institutions have begun to realize that they need to address in different ways the value systems that these cultures bring to an institution.

The change in seeing student discipline as a part of stu-dent development is really a concept of relationships. The purpose of student development seen in the context of law and order is an entirely different relationship than the rela-tionship of using student discipline as a means to educate students to specific values and behavior patterns. This change in relationship is partly due to institutions moving from an en loco parentis with students to understanding that students are stakeholders in the education process. This change in relationship is also the result of institutions mov-ing from measuring their quality by input and resources to that of educational results and outcomes. Increasingly, insti-tutions are realizing that results are the product of processes and systems. Student discipline is an integral part of these processes.

In this report, authored by Michael Dannells, professor of counseling and educational psychology and coordinator of the student personnel program at Kansas State University, student discipline is examined from a number of perspectives. After reviewing the history of student discipline, Dr. Dannells examines the characteristic of student offenders and what role institutions might play in this misconduct. Discipline issues such as the legal responsibility of the institution are detailed, as well as various models and practices institutions can use to make student discipline have as a major objective the educational development of a student.

The rules and regulations of an institution establish necessary boundaries that define the values and standards of the institution. The implementation process of student discipline codes should be consistent with these fundamental values and objectives. Student discipline as part of the education process should be designed and implemented in a way that will be a positive force in helping an institution achieve its long term education mission.

INTRODUCTION

Student Discipline—A Topic of Concern and Debate
Student discipline has been a topic of concern and debate throughout the history of American higher education; today is no exception. No other single topic is "such a dramatic reflection of our attitudes and assumptions about the nature of our students, our relationship to them, and our role in their development" (Dannells 1988, pp. 148-149). From the earliest dissatisfactions with paternalism (Rudolf 1962) to the recent controversies over hate speech versus First Amendment rights (Gibbs 1992), student conduct and institutional responses have vexed college faculty and administrators with a set of issues both fundamental and timely. What standards of behavior can colleges impose? How are those standards best communicated? By what processes should misconduct be adjudicated? If standards are broken, how should institutions respond? What is our overarching purpose in student discipline? How do we know when it is met?

Student discipline comprises a set of complex and interrelated issues that deserve careful examination and reasonable recommendations. It is the purpose of this monograph to provide both, with an eye toward new trends in responding to and preventing student misconduct, and in programs that avoid undue legalism, while enhancing student development and conflict resolution in furthering the institutional mission.

The subject of student discipline touches on many legal issues, many of which are noted herein; however, this report is not about the legal aspects of student discipline, and it makes no effort to be comprehensive in this regard. Other, comprehensive resources (see Kaplin and Lee 1995) are available to the reader. Also, this report is not intended to provide legal advice for individuals or their institutions. Some generalizations about the law related to the subject are presented, but they should not be relied upon in lieu of advice from competent legal counsel.

HISTORY OF STUDENT DISCIPLINE

The evolution of student discipline in American higher education mirrors, in many important respects, the historical development of American colleges and universities (Smith 1994). To understand student discipline today, an understanding and appreciation of its origins, the ways it has changed, and the events and forces that influenced those changes are required.

Student Discipline in the Colonial Colleges

The earliest American colleges were established by the colonies to ensure that their future religious and civic leaders would be "piously educated in good letters and manners" (Godbold in Rudolph 1962, p. 7), according to the sectarian principles of their founders. While the purposes of the original colonial colleges reflected denominational differences, they shared a set of nonsectarian educational and civic ends. To these ends, the students—almost all of whom were boys the age of today's high school students, some even younger —were subject to a curriculum and an authoritarian form of governance, that did not distinguish between mental and behavioral discipline, or between religious and intellectual training. While the academic, social, and moral aims of the college were virtually indistinguishable, and the context was clearly religious, dominated by Calvinist doctrine (Smith 1994), it was the influence of the English residential college, more than Puritanism, that shaped the colleges and their approach to matters of student behavior. The "collegiate way," defined by its residential nature, away from the distractions of the town, and "permeated by paternalism" (Rudolph 1962, p. 87), required rigorous and extensive regulation of conduct.

Fearing the unbridled expression of the natural depravity of their charges, the early colonial college trustees, presidents, and faculties set about shaping the moral character and social manners of their students through long and detailed codes of conduct and rigid scheduling. No portion of the day was unaccounted for, and no misbehavior was too small to go unrecognized and unpunished. In many ways, the view and treatment of the students and the atmosphere it produced "resembled a low-grade boys' boarding school straight out of the pages of Dickens" (Brubacher and Rudy 1976, p. 50). Students' lives were regulated in virtually every way—when they arose and retired, when and what they ate, what they wore, and how they behaved in and out of class, etc. Conduct was dictated by rule and monitored by the close attention of the president, the teachers, and the tutors. In the more serious cases, the president would share decisions with the board, which would hear the matter and rule on the appropriate punishment. Minor infractions were delegated to the faculty and later to the tutors. Punishments ranged from expulsion (which was communicated to the presidents of other colonial colleges to ensure the miscreant would not subsequently enroll at another school) to fatherly counseling. But flogging was the standard means of discipline, until 1718, when Harvard ceased its use. Flogging was followed by "boxing," "in which a bad boy was made to kneel at the feet of his tutor, who proceeded to smack him sharply on the ear" (Rudolph 1962, p. 27). Public reprimands and confessions ("degradation"), fines, loss of privileges, and extra assignments were common.

The warrant for this extensive supervision, and the harsh sanctions, arose from the authority vested in the board, which in turn was derived from the power of the colony. The colonists made laws that circumscribed the conduct of their youth and, at least in New England, they "empowered their governments to act *in loco parentis*" (Leonard 1956, p. 12). In fact, some colonial laws extended beyond parental authority, allowing for the possible punishment by death of children who willfully disobeyed, cursed, or struck their parents. In this light, and given the then-great distances and difficulties of travel, it is perhaps less surprising that the colonial colleges acted in the place of the parents in all things pertaining to the proper education and guidance of the youth in their charge, in accordance with the community and religious standards of the times. Thus:

> *students were forbidden to lie, steal, curse, swear, use obscene language, play at cards or dice, get drunk, frequent inns, associate with any person of bad reputation, commit fornication, fight cocks, call each other nicknames, buy, sell, or exchange anything, or be disrespectful, or tardy, or disorderly at public worship* (Leonard 1965, pp. 26-27).

The Early Federal Period to the Civil War
The long lists of proscribed behaviors and the stringent punishments at the colleges carried over into the newly formed

federation of states, but new forces were coming to bear on the repressive approach to discipline. One was democracy, itself. In an increasingly democratic society, "the strict, authoritarian, patriarchal family was making no headway in American life, and for colleges to insist on it was, for them, to fight the course of history" (Rudolph 1962, p. 104). The strict codes, usually borrowed from New England colleges, were especially difficult to apply in the South where the young college men knew such punishments were reserved for slaves (Brubacher and Rudy 1976).

The Collegiate Way required the country colleges, and of those "not-so-country," to build dormitories and dining halls, or commons. While the advantages of providing food and lodging, where there were few other alternatives, may have been obvious for the expansion of the college, and for the molding of the character and manners of the students, they also provided fertile ground for frustration, rebellion, strikes, and violent crime (Rudolph 1962). The clash of paternalistic methods of discipline combined. . .

> *with the spirit of liberty students exuded in the wake of the revolution . . . [resulted in] . . . a recurring pattern of student rebellion that lasted through the early decades of the nineteenth century. At most colleges, buildings were burned, professors were assaulted and sometimes killed, and students staged open rebellions in response to bad food, unilateral expulsions, and what they considered to be general abridgment of their rights* (Smith 1994, p. 79).

The dormitories and dining commons placed additional burdens of supervision on the faculty, who at most colleges lived on campus. Acting *in loco parentis*, the teachers and tutors were expected to patrol the dormitories, demand entrance, inspect all rooms for violations of the myriad rules, and to generally supervise the students, while quashing the seemingly ubiquitous food riots. Despite the help of student monitors, who were indispensable for the elaborate espionage systems that developed at some colleges, these duties became increasingly onerous and resented by the faculty (Leonard 1956; Rudolph 1962). Unlike their teaching counterparts at Oxford and Cambridge, who had handed over disciplinary matters to specialists during the 18th century, in America:

[f]aculty members remained saddled with the responsibility of enforcing all disciplinary regulations. They thus appeared in the guise of the students' natural enemies. Instead of separating the teaching and proctoring functions, American Colleges . . . made it practically impossible for students and professors to develop close and amicable relations (Brubacher and Rudy 1976, p. 42).

Through the period of the late 18th century, and the first half of the 19th century, despite—or perhaps as a result of—frequent student rebellions, punishments became generally milder, and persuasion and counseling emerged as a more common response to minor forms of student misconduct. As enrollments grew and the intellectual aims of the colleges broadened, the trustees, and then the presidents, gradually withdrew from direct and active involvement in disciplinary matters. During this period, the first disciplinary specialists were appointed from the faculty ranks, and it was these specialists who were the first persons to seriously employ counseling in working with troublesome students (Leonard 1956; Schetlin 1967). The earliest experiments in student self-government and discipline were tried, and though not particularly successful, the seeds of more participative forms of disciplinary systems, consonant with the democratic times, had been sown. In what she called "the years of expansion" (1812-1862), Leonard (1956) concluded that student conduct was much less violent than in earlier periods, while student-faculty relationships improved markedly. She credits both developments to the increasingly less intrusive forms of faculty supervision and the increased use of honor systems. This was also a time marked by the emergence of many organized student activities, including a variety of student-led societies; many of the literary, religious, music, social, and Greek-letter honor societies began during this period. Athletic clubs were formed on many campuses, and the new gymnastics movement imported from Germany flourished in the American college. Although these sorts of activities were not initially encouraged by the faculty, particularly in the more Puritan institutions, the release of youthful energies in such benign endeavors, compared to the earlier rebellions, and the "bitter enmity between faculty and students" (Brubacher and Rudy 1976, p.123) that characterized the preceding period. This must have come as a welcome relief to faculty and administration, who in the end tolerated, if not celebrated, the burgeoning extra curriculum.

The Post Civil War Period

This period has been characterized as one of "disciplinary enlightenment" (Smith 1994), a time when many forces conspired to reshape colleges' expectations and treatment of their students toward a more positive view of students as young adults capable of making decisions about their education and their conduct. Probably no one was more influential in this than Charles Eliot, the president of Harvard from 1869 to 1909. According to Brubacher and Rudy:

> Eliot held the view that a true university college should give its students three essentials; first, freedom of choice in studies; second, opportunity to win distinction in special lines of study; and finally, a system of discipline which imposes on the individual himself the main responsibility for guiding his conduct (1976, p. 112; emphasis added).

This view was to become common, and coupled with the elective principle and the expanding curriculum, it created a new atmosphere on the campus. In the first year of Eliot's term as president, Harvard ceased the practice of combining academic grades with delinquency demerits, the measure of "character," in the ranking of its students (Rudolph 1962).

The development in American universities of the scholarly ideal of the German universities, following the Civil War, left faculty increasingly disinclined to engage in disciplinary matters, or in student life in general. Faculty trained in the German tradition found the approach of faculty as monitors of student behavior demeaning to their role as research scholars. Meanwhile, at the state universities and urban schools, "the emphasis on utilitarian considerations and the spirit of democracy made the old-time authoritative and paternalistic approach seem increasingly out of place" (Brubacher and Rudy 1976, p. 124). In its place, a movement of "democratic humanization" flourished (Shaler 1889, cited in Smith 1994), despite resistance from the "old guard." Methods of rule enforcement and punishments became

The earliest experiments in student self-government and discipline were tried, and though not particularly successful, the seeds of more participative forms of disciplinary systems, consonant with the democratic times, had been sown.

more humane, and more concern was shown for the rights of the individual (Schetlin 1967).

As the faculty role in student discipline diminished in the late 19th century, the responsibility fell back to the President, who increasingly delegated it to specialists chosen from the faculty for their rapport with students, or to student groups in the form of student governments and honors systems (Leonard 1956; Schetlin 1967; Smith and Kirk 1971). These specialists came to be titled Deans of Men/Women, and later Deans of Students, and were the first professional student personnel workers, although they did not refer to themselves as such (Appleton, Briggs, and Rhatigan 1978). While the delegation of responsibility for student conduct to student groups and honor systems met with limited success (Brubacher and Rudy 1976), the Dean of Men/Women position became standard on most campuses by the early 1900s. Student discipline was not the sole purpose for the development of these positions, as is occasionally asserted in the literature. By the early 20th century, some colleges and most universities were "bifurcated," in that the intellectual life of the institution was largely independent from the actual experience of students, whose energies were devoted more to the extra curriculum (Brubacher and Rudy 1976). The early deans of men and women were designated to help students in this time when "much of higher education was jettisoning that responsibility" (Appleton et al. 1978, p. 12) by leading the way in efforts to reintegrate the curriculum and the extra curriculum, thereby not only restoring "a unified life to the American college, but also [reviving] the old-time college's concern for the nonintellectual side of the student's career" (Brubacher and Rudy 1976, p. 332). Student discipline was a part of this concern for the "whole student."

The early deans expanded on both the philosophy and practice of student discipline. Philosophically, they were humanistic, optimistic, and idealistic. They approached discipline with the ultimate goal of student self-control or self-discipline, and they used individualized and preventative methods in an effort to foster the development of the whole student (Clark 1915). Counseling became a popular form of corrective action (Fley 1964), and self-governance and student involvement in disciplinary systems were generally encouraged.

The Personnel Movement in the Early 20th Century

The origins of the student personnel movement emerged in the coalescence on campus of several other movements, including vocational guidance, applied psychology, educational psychology and measurement, and mental hygiene/ health. These are well chronicled elsewhere (Appleton et al. 1978; Brubacher and Rudy 1976; Fenske 1989) and are beyond the scope of this work. Nonetheless, this movement has relevance here because student discipline became a point of philosophical disagreement and separation between the early deans and the emerging student personnel specialists (Appleton et al. 1978; Knock 1985). The personnel specialists, whose work spanned a wider range of developmental services than the deans, "tended to view the deans' disciplining students as antithetical to their developmental efforts . . . and to regard the dean's role as a disciplinarian only in the sense of punishment. . . . This view separated the 'punishing' dean from the 'promoting' personnel worker" (Knock 1985, pp. 32-33; see also Brady 1965). As campuses grew and became more heterogeneous, so grew the deans' disciplinary work, and with it, their image as "the bad guys," more interested in control and punishment than in human development, which the personnel specialists claimed as their own. This negative image of the early deans, and the unnecessary schism that developed in the nascent field of student personnel work, is all the more unfortunate because records of the early meetings of the deans show they spoke of their work in terms of "character formation," "citizenship training," and "moral and ethical development," and not in terms of punishment and control (Appleton et al. 1978).

From World War II to Today: Changing Students, Changing Rules

The end of World War II and the GI Bill brought to college huge numbers of older and more worldly students who "could not digest the traditional palliatives served up by the dean to justify student conduct regulation and discipline" (Smith and Kirk 1971), but their academic orientation and skills in organizational survival, learned in military service, kept them from forcing a crisis. College students in the decade following WWII are often characterized as the "silent generation" (Brubacher and Rudy 1976), and the period is generally regarded as the calm before the storm of the 1960s. During this time, increasing emphasis was placed on rehabilitation of student offenders, and professionally trained counselors were given more responsibility in discipline. Hearing boards composed of both faculty/staff and students were increasingly established and utilized (Sims 1971), although "the rise of student participation in disciplinary systems was accompanied by significant debate over the efficacy of students as disciplinarians" (Smith 1994, p. 83).

The student revolution of the 1960s and early 1970s, has been described as "the most portentous upheaval in the whole history of American student life" (Brubacher and Rudy 1976, p. 349). Many forces, including the civil rights movement, the anti-Vietnam war movement, increasing tolerance in judicial decisions on moral issues such as pornography, the lowering of the age of majority, and the student rights movement itself, conspired to change colleges' expectations of their students and methods of discipline. Campus disruptions became common and sometimes violent as students demonstrated for peace, freedom from conscription, freedom from parietal rules, and for greater involvement in campus governance. Student disciplinary hearings themselves were often the stage for dissent of one form or another.

The 1960s left two enduring legacies related to campus discipline: First, *in loco parentis*, or what remained of it, was dealt the apparently fatal blow; and second, the litigation about disciplinary procedures that began in that period continues today (Smith 1994). "Fundamentally, the basis for the doctrine *in loco parentis* had been disintegrating for some time" (Brubacher and Rudy 1976, p. 352). As early as 1957, the issue of students' constitutional rights in dismissal hearings at public institutions was raised (see Seavey 1957). In addition, less control-oriented methods of parenting and a rapidly changing, more worldly, diverse, and mature student body had contributed to the breakdown of collegiate paternalism. The ratification of the Twenty-Sixth Amendment, which lowered the voting age to 18, and prompted the lowering of the age of majority to 18, for most purposes in most states (Kaplin and Lee 1995), substantially contributed to the movement away from viewing the student-institutional relationship as *in loco parentis* to a more contractual and consumerist view.

Federal court intervention into the disciplinary process of public institutions in the 1960s centered on students' First and Fourteenth Amendment rights. This intervention marked the beginning of a rush on many campuses to adopt legalistic, adversarial procedures that mirrored those of our criminal system, and triggered the ongoing struggle between the student development position and the legalistic position (Smith 1994). Today, most campuses use a bipartite system of discipline that employs informal and educationally oriented methods in minor cases. In serious cases, especially those that might result in dismissal, more formal procedures are used, which are designed to protect the civil liberties of students. These are addressed in a later section of this report.

After a careful analysis of the undergraduate experience at American colleges and universities, Ernest Boyer, then President of the Carnegie Foundation for the Advancement of Teaching, wrote:

> *What we found particularly disturbing is the ambivalence college administrators feel about their overall responsibility for student behavior. Most of the college leaders with whom we spoke had an unmistakable sense of unease—or was it anxiety? Many were not sure what standards to expect or require. Where does the responsibility of the college begin and end? Where is the balance to be struck between students' personal "rights" and institutional concerns. . . . Unclear about what standards to maintain and the principles by which student life should be judged, many administrators seek to ignore rather than confront the issues* (1987, p. 203).

Summary
Student discipline was an important part of American higher education in its early history. In the colonial colleges, it was a central function, inseparable from the basic mission of the institution to further the intellectual and moral welfare of students. With the introduction of the German university model, faculty were generally relieved (both functionally and psychologically) from the burden of student discipline, which had always been a source of distance and dissension between them and their students. As colleges grew and became more complex, specialists emerged to handle much of the administration of the college, including student disci-

pline, which was typically assigned to the Dean of Men and later to the Dean of Students. Within the student personnel profession, student discipline has been a source of disagreement on such issues as "punishment versus development" and "process (especially legal) versus outcome (education)."

Student discipline has been a "hot potato" in the history of American higher education. Once a central function, now it is peripheral and controversial. Today, institutional leaders continue to show ambivalence about it, and it would not be an exaggeration to say that many, perhaps most, wish it just went away.

PRESENT-DAY CONCERNS ABOUT STUDENT MISCONDUCT AND CRIME ON CAMPUS

Concerns about student misconduct are as old as higher education itself, dating back to the earliest European universities. In the United States, "the riots of the early 19th century,
the mayhem of the 1960s, and campus violence in the 1990s
indicate that student misconduct is an enduring reality—not
a temporal problem—that demands continual attention"
(Smith 1994, p. 84; Smith and Fossey 1995). The concern of
student misconduct is a given, but underlying much of the
discussion in recent years is an assumption that student behavior is somehow worse today than in previous eras. It is
common to hear such claims as "student conduct problems
are on the increase . . . and require more time and attention
by university officials" (Dalton and Healy 1984, p. 19), yet
hard evidence to support this seems to be lacking (Dannells
1991). The primary difficulty in research on student conduct
over time is the lack of baseline data. Anecdotal information
about student behavior in the past abounds (Brubacher and
Rudy 1976; Rudolph 1962), and it certainly lends perspective
to the subject, yet it does not permit the kind of longitudinal
comparison necessary to support recent rhetoric about how
bad student behavior has become. Perhaps the information
now required of colleges and universities under the Student
Right-to-Know and Campus Security Act of 1990 will, over
time, help to remedy this lack of baseline data and help re-
searchers examine the claim of increasing crime on campus.
Campus crime statistics must be used with caution in this
context, since they include only criminal acts of students, as
well as nonstudents.

While there may be doubt as to whether or not college
student misconduct has changed over time, today's high
level of concern about student behavior and campus crime
is undeniable. One of most widely read reports that addresses this subject is the Carnegie Foundation for the
Advancement of Teaching's (1990) *Campus Life: In Search of
Community.* The Carnegie Foundation reported on a 1989
survey of college presidents and senior student affairs officers conducted jointly by the American Council on
Education and the National Association of Student Personnel
Administrators:

> *While campuses are safer than city streets, the
> frequency of criminal acts, for many colleges, is an-
> other cause of worry. Indeed, one in four of the student*

affairs officers responding to our survey say that the number of reported crimes on their campus has increased over the last five years. Forty-three percent of those responding at research and doctorate-granting institutions believe the number of reported crimes on campus has increased over the last five years. One liberal arts college in our study reported a 27 percent rise in vandalism in just one year. Thefts are considered a problem by about two-thirds of the presidents at doctorate-granting institutions; 38 percent of liberal arts college presidents; and 44 percent at two-year institutions (Carnegie Foundation 1990, p. 40).

On the matter of campus crime statistics including non-students, the Carnegie Foundation noted:

Further, contrary to conventional wisdom, most criminal activity on campus is committed not by "outsiders" but by students. Students are, according to a recent report [National Campus Violence Survey, General Report 1988], responsible for 78 percent of sexual assaults, 52 percent of physical assaults, two-thirds of strong-arm robberies, more than 90 percent of arsons, and 85 percent of incidents of vandalism (p. 42).

Sloan (1994) reviewed the findings of the 1990 U.S. Congressional Hearings on Campus Crime and reported that in the period 1985-1989, campus crime steadily increased; more than 80 percent of campus crime involved students as both perpetrators and victims, and 95 percent of campus crime involved the use of alcohol or other drugs. Sloan (1994), in his research on data collected by Ordovensky, found that in the academic year 1989-1990, on 481 campuses with 3,000 or more students, there were 195,000 reported offenses—64 percent, burglary or theft; 19 percent, vandalism; 11 percent, alcohol or drug related, and less than 2 percent, serious violent crime. He calculated the rate of reported crime for that period at 33 offenses per 1,000 students.

While "[m]ost studies of campus crime show that colleges are safer than the communities around them," the data collected for a recent *Chronicle of Higher Education* report showed a "continuing increase in the number of violent crimes" on campuses with enrollments of more than 5,000

(Lederman 1995, p. A41). With such reports, the pressure mounts for colleges to respond with preventative measures, criminal prosecution, and disciplinary action.

Reporting on another national survey of chief student affairs officers (CSAOs), conducted during the 1991-1992 academic year, Gallagher, Harmon, and Lingenfelter (1994) found that two-thirds of CSAOs reported an increase in the number of students with severe psychological problems on their campuses:

> *Sixty-six percent cited an increase in women reporting sexual harassment, 68 percent noted an increase in acquaintance rape cases, and 48 percent indicated dating violence had increased. Also, 11 percent indicated illicit drug use had increased over the past five years; 40 percent said alcohol use had increased; 86 percent noted an increase in administrative attention to alcohol abuse, and 34.5 percent of the CSAOs reported they had to intervene in one or more stalking cases during the past year* (pp. 40,42).

Regardless of whether or not campus crime is actually increasing, we now have the beginning of baseline data on the matter. Smith and Fossey (1995) noted that the first round of national reporting in 1992, under the Student Right-to-Know and Campus Security Act, included "30 murders, nearly 1,000 rapes, 1,800 robberies from persons, 32,127 burglaries, and 8,981 stolen motor vehicles." They also suggested that the number of actual offenses is probably much larger for three reasons. First, not all offenses are reported; only about one-half of all felonies in the United States are reported and the percentage of misdemeanors is even smaller. Second, the figures reported include only on-campus crimes and do not include those that involve students outside the formal boundaries of the campus. Third, despite the federal reporting requirements, "some observers continue to suspect that, at least at some institutions, crime statistics may be shaded downward or intentionally understated by image-conscious campus authorities" (p. 13).

In addition to the numbers of relatively "traditional" crimes on campus, Smith and Fossey (1995) noted concern about three new types of campus violence: (1) Courtship violence and inter-roommate violence, which demand in-

... findings of the 1990 U.S. Congressional Hearings on Campus Crime [and] reported that in the period 1985-1989, campus crime steadily increased ...

creasing vigilance of all campus agencies that may note the signs of abuse like those seen in community shelters and hospitals; (2) violence against resident assistants, who seem to be ready targets and need protection from verbal abuse, threats, and actual physical harm; and (3) retaliatory abuse directed at those who make judicial complaints against other students.

> *Criminal violence, theft, and vandalism clearly pervade contemporary American campus life. What would have been called student high jinks a few years ago are now being recognized for the exploitive and damaging criminal behavior that they are. The inclination of some administrators to ignore the problem, in the hope either that it is not really there, or that it will go away, is no longer reasonable or responsible* (Smith and Fossey 1995, p. 20).

Smith and Fossey urged the construction and application of responses that include:

> *(1) finding ways of persuading offenders not to commit offenses, if possible; (2) making it difficult or impossible for the offender to do it if he or she is not dissuaded; and (3) providing support and rehabilitation systems for both victims and offenders in those cases where the offense was not prevented. Education has a key role to play in all three aspects* (1995, p. 21).

For a more thorough treatment of campus crime and for specific strategies for addressing campus violence, in addition to *Crime on Campus* (Smith and Fossey 1995), *Responding to Violence on Campus* (Sherill and Siegel 1989) is recommended, as well as Pezza (1995) and Pezza and Bellotti (1995).

Demands for More Supervision of Students

Some may find it ironic that not long after the celebration of the 25th anniversary of the "Joint Statement on Rights and Freedoms of Students" (Bryan and Mullendore 1992), and "[h]aving moved from strict control over student conduct to treating students as adults, subject to much less control, institutions now are being pressed to take more responsibility for students' behavior" (Pavela 1992, p. B1). Also, the same consumer-protection movement that aided the progress for students' rights left students with concurrent liabilities, including taking more responsibility for themselves and making it more difficult for them to hold colleges responsible for injuries suffered at the hands of other students. Regarding student-consumer protection statutes, such as the Student Right-to-Know and Campus Security Act, Pavela (1992) observed that:

> *frequently [they] go well beyond setting guidelines for reporting information to students; they often contain explicit or implicit requirements that specific disciplinary policies—like restrictions against underage drinking—be adopted, enforced, and monitored by colleges to protect students and members of the public* (pp. B1-2).

Besides legislation, other social and economic forces have conspired to pressure colleges to take greater responsibility for their students' behavior, whether on or off campus, "at the worst possible time" (Pavela 1992, p. B2). There is a need for deans and presidents to take the creative lead in setting and enforcing standards of student behavior that will result in more responsible and civil student conduct (Pavela 1992).

Summary

Despite a "conventional wisdom" that college student misbehavior is worse now than in the past, and media reports of increasing campus crime, reliable evidence about student conduct over time is scarce. Still, present-day concerns about student conduct are reasonable and warranted, especially as misconduct takes the form of increasingly abusive/exploitative interpersonal conduct such as domestic violence, date/acquaintance rape, and hate speech. Public concern about campus crime, the current climate of "accountability," and an increasingly litigious society are external forces that contribute to the importance of student discipline today and require positive and creative leadership in this challenging area.

THE VARIOUS DEFINITIONS AND PURPOSES OF STUDENT DISCIPLINE

Student discipline has long been a painful and controversial topic, due in no small measure to disagreement over its meaning and purpose. It has been variously defined as: the internal control of behavior, or the virtue of *self-discipline*; the external control of behavior, or *punishment*; and the *process of reeducation* or rehabilitation (Appleton et al. 1978). The evolution of discipline in the history of American higher education has been from the external to the internal (Wrenn 1949), with the emphasis in the 1960s and 1970s on the process itself and on "judicial systems." Most recently, there has been increasing interest and attention to the moral development of students and to the application of human development theories to that end (see Boots 1987; Dannells 1988; Dalton and Healy 1984; Pavela 1985).

Two other views of discipline may affect its actual practice on any given campus (Dannells 1977). One is pure intellectualism, which holds that the college's duty is to train the intellect and that it should have no part in moral, social, ethical, or character formation (or reformation). The other, which often accompanies the pure intellectualism view, is called the legalistic or strict constructionist view, and it holds that the college may discipline students as a means of protecting the educational environment.

It seems reasonable to postulate that, in fact, two or more of the various views of student discipline may coexist on a college campus at any one time. Although punishment for punishment's sake is certainly disavowed in the academy, there is no doubting its usefulness as a means of influencing behavior, either for the student's sake or for the institution. In the process of moral development, Pavela offers a rationale for the use of retributive punishment as a means for reaffirming personal responsibility (1985, pp. 45-52). An argument against a disciplinary system, based on retributive punishment is made by Carrington (1971). Likewise, most campuses probably have faculty who see little or no place for student discipline—such is the legacy of the influence of the Continental research university.

Theories on the Authority to Discipline

Just as there are several views of what constitutes student discipline, there are several theories and legal doctrines that describe the institution's authority and the scope of its role or "jurisdiction" (Ratliff 1972). They include: *in loco parentis,*

---

contract, educational purpose, statutory, constitutional, fiduciary, and status. A brief review of each is justified because, as Stoner and Cerminara (1990) said, "the legal relationship between a college or a university and its students has never fit neatly within one legal doctrine" (pp. 89-90).

In loco parentis, literally "in the place of a parent or instead of a parent," is an early English common law doctrine that is generally thought to have been first applied to the college-student relationship in the case of *Gott v. Berea College* (1913), although it was used in the case of *The People v. Wheaton College* (Illinois Supreme Court 1866), cited in Hoekema (1994). This doctrine viewed the institution as having the rights and duties of parents with respect to student conduct and welfare, therefore allowing it great latitude in the disciplinary process, and "permitted the institution to exert almost untrammeled authority over students' lives" (Kaplin and Lee 1995, p. 5). Although this doctrine was formalized into law "long after the original relationship was abandoned in practice" (Appleton et al. 1978, p. 25), it is commonly used to describe the relationship for most of the pre-1960s history of American higher education. By the late 1960s, the obvious difficulties, both in law and in actual practice, were well apparent, and the doctrine as it had been applied to college student discipline was generally considered impractical and untenable, if not simply dead (Dannells, 1977). What, if anything, has taken its place in guiding institutional policy, vis-a-vis students' non-academic conduct, is unclear and will be the subject for further consideration later in this report.

The *contract theory* defines the relationship of student to college as a contractual one, the terms of which are articulated in the college catalog, other publications (such as class schedules and "viewbooks"), and oral addenda made by college officials. The student accepts the colleges' conduct rules and academic regulations by signing enrollment papers. For all but the recent history of American higher education, "[t]he institution was given virtually unlimited power to dictate the contract terms, and the contact, once made, was construed heavily in the institution's favor" (Kaplin and Lee 1995, p. 6). Once restricted almost exclusively to private institutions and to academic affairs, this theory has been used increasingly as students have come to be viewed as adult consumers capable of entering into contracts, such as those for campus housing, with institutions of all types. As noted previously, the lowering of the age of majority in the 1970s affected the application of this theory in most states. Today, in most states, college students are considered legal adults for the purpose of entering into contracts, but since state-to-state variance exists, college administrators and their legal counsel are encouraged to consult their state's law in this regard (Kaplin and Lee 1995).

The *educational purpose theory* defines the student-institutional relationship as an educational function and limits its authority to behavior that is related to the institution's pursuit of its educational mission. This view is generally considered by educators (but certainly not by legal authorities) to be the only realistic and justifiable basis for disciplinary authority today, especially given the current highly litigious climate. It requires colleges and universities to be explicit and intentional about their educational goals; it allows institutions to establish rules to protect the educational environment; and "it protects the institution from unwanted court intrusion by recognizing that the courts have historically adopted a policy of nonintervention, or judicial restraint, in matters that are legitimately part of the educational enterprise" (Dannells 1988, p. 134).

The *statutory theory* refers to the granting of disciplinary authority to the institution or its governing board through legislation by local, state, or federal government. The legislation may grant disciplinary authority directly to the faculty; it may grant it to the board with explicit or implicit authorization to delegate it to the faculty; or it may be a general grant of power without mention of discipline. Some writers have claimed that this theory is the only practical legal basis for disciplinary power (see Bakken 1968; Snoxell 1965), while others have claimed it has won only limited support in the courts (see Ratliff 1972).

The *constitutional theory* describes the legal limitations on public institutions' power to enact rules that affect individual liberties. The nature and extent of the limitations imposed by the First and Fourteenth Amendments to the federal Constitution will be detailed in later sections on due process and on hate speech.

The last two theories of disciplinary authority are worthy of only passing mention because they have seldom been relied on by the courts (Ratliff 1972). The *fiduciary or trust theory* holds that the institution assumes the fiduciary function and acts for the benefit of the student in "all matters relevant between them" (Seavey 1957, p. 1407, n. 3; see also Fowler 1984). The *status, custom, or usage theory* views the relationship as inherent in the status of the parties and that the custom (rule) derives as a matter of tradition or commonly understood institutional policy or practice. Kaplan and Lee provide a description of how this source of authority relates to the contract theory (1995, pp. 16-18).

The Extent of Institutional Jurisdiction

There are two basic jurisdictional issues faced by colleges and universities in student discipline (Stein 1972). First, in instances where both institutional rules and criminal law may apply, should the institution take internal action, seek external (criminal) sanctions, or both? Related to this conundrum is the matter of double jeopardy. Second, should the institution concern itself with off-campus behavior?

The answer to both questions—in the affirmative—resides in the educational purpose theory of viewing the student-institutional relationship. As Kaplin and Lee (1995) pointed out, it is common for codes of conduct to proscribe misconduct, "whether or not the misconduct violates civil or criminal laws, and whether or not the misconduct occurs on campus" (p. 457). Central to both is whether the behavior in question directly relates to the educational mission or to the welfare of the campus community.

Students have occasionally argued that to be subject to both institutional discipline and to be tried on a criminal charge for the same behavior constitutes double jeopardy; i.e., that they have been tried twice for the same offense, in violation of the Fifth Amendment to the Constitution. However, it is well established in the law that the prohibition against double jeopardy applies only to successive *criminal* proceedings, which campus actions, based on violations of institutional rules rather than criminal statutes, are not. Kaplin and Lee (1995) further pointed out that the courts have generally rejected attempts by students to avoid campus proceedings because they may violate the student's privilege against self-incrimination. However, in cases that may involve evidential difficulties, like a charge of rape, campuses are generally cautioned to defer to criminal proceedings that are better designed to handle such things as scientific evidence and complex or conflicting testimony.

What, in fact, do colleges and universities claim as their jurisdiction in matters of student conduct? We know that for most of the American history, in keeping with its mission of character formation, the academy concerned itself with all student behavior. Students' off-campus conduct was as important as their on-campus behavior, and all behavior was "educationally related." In this century, the movement was clearly away from that position toward more permissiveness and less control, at least until recent years when we have witnessed some evidence of increasing regulation of students' out-of-class lives (Hoekema 1994; Pavela 1992). In a longitudinal study comparing disciplinary policies and practices from 1978 to 1988, Dannells (1990) found that four-year colleges and universities had indeed broadened the scope of their disciplinary authority. Over that period the percentage of those schools that considered all student behavior, both on- and off-campus, increased significantly (from 35.7 percent to 45.7 percent), while the percentage of those that were concerned with only on-campus behavior decreased significantly (from 56.4 percent to 43.3 percent). In a related study, Dannells (1991) reported evidence suggesting that campus officials were more likely in 1988, than in 1978, to refer cases involving violations of the law, particularly sexual assault, to the civil authorities. So it appears that over this 10-year period, campuses in general both broadened their scope of jurisdiction and were more inclined to defer to criminal prosecution in more serious cases. This change over time might be attributable to the movement toward victims' rights, which in many states and local juristictions has made the criminal process less onerous for the alleged student-victim. Another influence may be the increasing realization on the part of campus administrators of the complexity and evidentiary issues of such cases, and the limitations of campus judicial systems in attempting to deal with them.

Students have occasionally argued that to be subject to both institutional discipline and to be tried on a criminal charge for the same behavior constitutes double jeopardy.

Without *in loco parentis,* how is a college or university to decide its scope of disciplinary authority? In his thoughtful and challenging book, *Campus Rules and Moral Community: In Place of In Loco Parentis,* David Hoekema (1994), an ethicist and professor of philosophy, made the case that:

> *the death of* in loco parentis *has spelled the end of any clear or coherent understanding of the college's responsibility for students' moral and social life. Unable to*

*play the role of parent, no longer prescribing bedtimes
or enforcing a moral code, the institution has effectively
withdrawn from the field of morality and character
formation* (p. 18).

The observation by the Carnegie Foundation for the
Advancement of Teaching (1990) that "today many [colleges]
are not sure where the oversight responsibility of the institution begins and ends," supports Hoekema's contention that
most colleges lack a clear focus in their approach to student
discipline (p. 37).

Summary
Multiple definitions, purposes, philosophies, and legal theories may be used to frame the practice of student disciplinary affairs. Most recently, with the demise of *in loco
parentis*, coupled with increasing demands for supervision,
the need to fashion an approach that meets the educational
purpose of the institution, while recognizing the rights of
students, has taken on new significance. Institutions need to
carefully consider their purpose(s) for engaging in student
discipline and not just react to outside pressures.

WHO MISBEHAVES AND WHY?

Characteristics of Student Offenders

According to Van Kuren and Creamer (1989), little is known about the origins of college student disciplinary problems, and what is known is based on theoretical descriptions of demographic and personality characteristics of student offenders. Tracey, Foster, Perkins and Hillman (1979) further criticized this body of research (Bazik and Meyering 1965; Lenning 1970; Tisdale and Brown 1965; Williamson, Jorve and Lagerstedt-Knutson 1952; Work 1969) on the basis of methodological problems and a lack of generalization from studies done in the 1960s (or earlier) to today's students. But based on the more recent studies by Janosik, Davis, and Spencer (1985) and Tracey et al. (1979), it is possible to demographically describe the bulk of student disciplinary offenders. Not surprisingly, most students who become involved in campus discipline difficulties are men, and most often, they are younger, usually in their freshman or sophomore year. These young men are more likely to live on campus (where their behavior is more closely monitored) than off-campus, and to live in larger residence halls. Studies that have compared offenders and nonoffenders on scholastic ability, grades, and major have had equivocal or conflicting results. The research on the demographics of students who engage in academic dishonesty will be addressed later in this report; however, it should be noted that cheating is one area where the proportion of women is increasing (Kibler, Cole, McCabe, Olson, Pavela and Richardson 1995).

The body of research on personality characteristics of offenders, which tends to be quite old, is fairly consistent and may not be as subject to generational differences as demographic studies. Again, the results are not surprising: Student disciplinary offenders in the 1950s and 1960s may be described as having been immature and lacking in impulse control, aggressive, less well socialized, hedonistic, and more likely to have difficulties in interpersonal relationships.

Most recently, Van Kuren and Creamer (1989) found that nonoffenders were more likely to have a parent or parents with a college degree than were offenders, which they suggested might be a function of anticipatory socialization by college-educated parents. They found that "students who had positive feelings about the institution, in general, were less likely to be offenders" (p. 264). More specifically, they found that:

*students who perceive a sense of helpfulness, encour-
agement, support, and openness on the part of other
students or faculty and administrators and feel that
they are making progress in acquiring career skills and
knowledge have a more positive outlook about the institution that, in turn, decreases their chances of becoming offenders* (p. 264).

The work of Van Kuren and Creamer is noteworthy in that it
tested a causal model and is based on person-environment
fit theories.

Sources of Student Misconduct:
Why Do Students Misbehave?

The sources of student misconduct may be divided into
those that reside outside the student, and those that are intrapersonal. What constitutes student misconduct is, of
course, a function of the goal(s) of the discipline program
and the nature and number of rules that follow from it (Foley
1947; Seward 1961; Williamson 1956, 1961; Williamson and
Foley 1949; Wrenn 1949). Likewise, the full array of campus
conditions will influence the frequency and nature of student
misconduct. For example, a residential campus with mostly
traditional-aged students could be expected to have a higher
incidence of misconduct than a nonresidential campus with
largely nontraditionally-aged commuter students.

Intrapersonal origins of student misconduct may be subcat-
egorized as nonpathological and pathological. Nonpathological misbehavior may be viewed as stemming from a lack of
information or understanding, or from inadequate or incom-
plete development, once generally referred to as immaturity
or natural adolescent mischievousness and "excess energy"
(Williamson 1956). Pathological origins of student misconduct
have drawn more attention in recent years, as psychopathology in college students seems to be on the rise (Dannells and
Stuber 1992) and because of the apparent increase in frequency of behaviors such as sexual harassment, acquaintance
rape, dating and domestic violence, alcohol abuse, and "stalk-
ing" (Gallagher, Harmon and Lingenfelter 1994).

Alcohol and Student Misconduct

The consumption of alcohol by college students and its relationship to problematic student conduct has been an issue in

American colleges and universities since the first colonial colleges. References to drunk and disorderly conduct, sometimes resulting in full-scale rioting, assaults on townspersons and members of the campus community, and even occasional shootings, are often found in the detailed histories of American institutions of higher education. Although the use of alcohol by college students in recent years may actually be on the decline (Hanson 1995), there is little doubt that alcohol abuse is still a serious problem and that it creates other behavior problems on college campuses.

Contemporary college administrators are clearly concerned with student alcohol abuse, especially as it affects others and the campus environment. In its survey of college and university presidents, the Carnegie Foundation (1990) found that two-thirds of them rated alcohol abuse a "moderate" to "major" problem on their campus. Anderson and Gadaleto (1991), cited in Hanson and Engs (1995) found that administrators believe alcohol is increasingly involved in damage to campus property, in violations of campus policy, and in violent behavior. A recent survey of 17,592 students at over 140 colleges (Wechsler, Deutsch and Dowdall 1995) has raised awareness about binge drinking by college students and heightened concern about the impact of that behavior on others. At campuses where binge drinking is common, 87 percent of the non-binge drinkers who lived on campus reported being adversely affected by others' binge drinking. Gehring noted that, according to a recent study conducted by an insurance company that covers several national fraternities, "94 percent of the sexual abuse claims against the fraternities it insures are alcohol related" (1996, p. 5).

Efforts on college campuses to influence student alcohol consumption through alcohol education programs, and to respond to alcohol-related disciplinary violations, are common. In addition to the usual disciplinary sanctions (expulsion, suspension, probation, fines, etc.), alcohol (and other drug) related policy violations are frequently met with assessment and educational responses such as alcohol/drug evaluation, referral to counseling, required attendance at educational programs, and/or taking part in self-help groups, e.g., Alcoholics Anonymous (Consolvo 1995). But the efficacy of campus alcohol policies has been questioned by the research of Hanson and Engs (1995), who found "institutional alcohol policies and practices had no discernible effect on drinking patterns and problems reported by students" (p. 110). In addition to several recommendations about shaping more effective alcohol education programs (in rejection of the "control of consumption" model that dominates in this area), they made two suggestions directly related to student discipline policies:

- *Systematic efforts should be made to clarify and empha-size the distinction between acceptable and unacceptable drinking.*
- *Unacceptable drinking behavior should be strongly sanc-tioned, both legally and socially. It is important that intox-ication not be accepted as an excuse for otherwise unacceptable behavior (p. 112).*

A complete review of the complex problems associated with alcohol (and other drug) use and abuse in college students is well beyond the scope of this report. For an entry into the literature on it, the lengthy reference list in Hanson and Engs (1995) is recommended.

Summary
Although our understanding of students who get into disci-plinary problems is based too much on studies done before 1980, we have a fairly clear and consistent profile: Immature, impulsive young men, most often freshmen and sophomores, who have not developed positive feelings to-ward the institution and who very likely were engaged in alcohol use or abuse at the time of the incident.

ACADEMIC DISHONESTY

Perhaps no other behavior strikes as directly at the core of the values of the academy as academic dishonesty. The search for truth and the discovery and transmission of knowledge require a faithfulness to the principles of honesty and integrity:

> *A tradition of learning and scholarship that stresses conscientious scholarly endeavor and scrupulous regard for the academic efforts and contributions of others stands at the foundation of our institutions of higher learning. By virtue of this tradition, the college or university is concerned not simply with imparting knowledge and ideas, but also with instilling a sense of integrity about academic work in its students. . . . The prevalence of academic dishonesty represents failure on the part of the college or university to achieve fundamental educational objectives* (Bowers 1964, p. 1).

Many are injured when a student engages in academic dishonesty. For the student in question, cheating obviously reflects a failure to master or communicate the mastery of the subject matter; it may obscure the failure to acquire necessary academic skills in studying, problem solving, test taking, researching, and/or writing; and it certainly represents a lack of ethical and moral development. Other students are disadvantaged by the cheater who gains unfair advantage in grading, by the loss of confidence and faith in the grading system, and by the erosion of the trust of faculty in all students. "On the campus at which academic dishonesty prevails, the honest student will be deprived of the best setting for intellectual growth and the development of academic integrity" (Bowers 1964, p. 2). The efforts of faculty to transmit knowledge and teach independent, critical thinking are likewise frustrated. It creates problems for the administration, which must devote institutional resources to the adjudication of charges of academic dishonesty, and which must be concerned with the potential for damaging publicity for the institution. Virtually every constituent of the academy is negatively affected by academic dishonesty.

Here are four examples in which "[w]idespread academic dishonesty poses a substantial threat to the educational enterprise" and beyond the campus:

- *A campus climate that appears to be tolerant of academic dishonesty may have the perverse effect of encouraging students who did not cheat in secondary school to adopt such a practice in college and throughout their lives. Such an outcome is the antithesis of what the college and university experience is designed to accomplish.*

- *Apparent faculty indifference to academic dishonesty communicates to students that the values of integrity and honesty are not sufficiently important to justify any serious effort to enforce them. This is a potentially devastating moral example for a generation of students who long for a sense of structure, are increasingly committed to improving society, and wish to be associated with a community of values.*

- *Most students are justifiably outraged when faculty and staff members appear to ignore obvious cases of cheating or plagiarism. Such feelings, should they become prevalent, will damage any sense of community on campus and alienate some of the very best students from the institution.*

- *Academic dishonesty deceives those who may eventually depend on the knowledge and integrity of our graduates* (Gehring and Pavela 1994, pp. 6-7).

Academic dishonesty may be defined as "forms of cheating and plagiarism which result in students giving or receiving unauthorized assistance in an academic exercise or receiving credit for work which is not their own" (Kibler, Nuss, Paterson and Pavela 1988, p. 1). Here is a commonly-used list, including definitions of those forms:

Cheating—*intentionally using or attempting to use unauthorized materials, information, or study aids in any academic exercise. The term academic exercise includes all forms of work submitted for credit or hours.*

Fabrication—*intentional or unauthorized falsification or invention of any information or citation in an academic exercise.*

Facilitating academic dishonesty—*intentionally or knowingly helping or attempting to help another to violate a provision of the institutional code of academic integrity.*

Plagiarism—*the deliberate adoption or reproduction of ideas or words or statements of another person as one's own without acknowledgement* (Kibler et al. 1988, pp. 1-2).

These definitions appear broad enough to include "old" forms of academic dishonesty, like using "crib sheets" in taking a test, as well as "newer, high tech" forms, such as using programmable wrist watches to hold and display information in a testing situation or using computer "hacking" to gain unauthorized access to faculty test files or to grade records.

Academic dishonesty is hardly a new problem; it has attracted the attention of college officials probably since the beginning of higher education, and it has been an area of scholarly inquiry for most of this century (Kibler 1993b). Some research (e.g., Ludeman 1988) and media reports (e.g., Collison 1990) have suggested that academic dishonesty is, and has been for several decades, on the increase, yet little or no empirical evidence is available to support this popular notion. The recent research of McCabe and Bowers (1994) indicates that, at least over the period 1963-1993, the percentage of students who admit to some form of cheating has been fairly stable.

... cited studies that show "between 40 percent and 90 percent of all college students cheat.

> *Student cheating has been the subject of much research, but most studies have focused on a single campus and yield little insight into general patterns of student cheating. In addition, there is a shortage of data that help us understand how student cheating has changed over time* (McCabe and Trevino 1996, p. 29).

Estimates of the incidence of academic dishonesty vary widely from campus to campus and from study to study. Kibler (1993a) cited several research studies that found frequencies as low as 23 percent to as high as 75 percent of students who admitted to having engaged in at least one instance of academic dishonesty. May and Loyd (1993, p. 125) cited studies that show "between 40 percent and 90 percent of all college students cheat." McCabe and Trevino (1993, p. 523) noted "prior studies report that anywhere from 13 percent to 95 percent of college students engage in some form of academic dishonesty." McCabe and Pavela (1993, p. 340) reported that 20 percent of students "can be classified as repetitive test cheaters," and Kibler et al. (1995) noted that recidivism seems to be on the increase. Genereux and McLeod (1995) recently found that 83 percent of one institution's students had engaged in some form of cheating while in college, and that the two most common forms were giving (58 percent) and getting (49 percent) test questions before an examination.

Any attempt to generalize widely diverse estimates to all college students is problematic for two reasons. First, the incidence of cheating no doubt varies from school to school. Second, the data of the various studies that have been conducted are not comparable because they are derived from different questions, using different definitions, asked in different ways, and asked of different types of students.

Even though we lack hard evidence of the general frequency of the problem, or if it is increasing, there can be no doubt that academic dishonesty is a serious concern at most colleges and universities. This concern may be especially reasonable in light of new computer and networking technology, which may make some forms of cheating harder to detect. As Lynn Smith, Director of the University of Manitoba's office of student advocacy was recently quoted in *High-tech Cheating*:

> *Computer networking opens up a whole new territory for downloading files off the Internet and CD-ROMS— material that is fairly fresh and hasn't been seen in a lot of places before—that some students will try to pass off as their own* (1995).

Why Do Students Cheat?

Why do students cheat? This deceptively simple question may be answered by considering student motives, student characteristics, and institutional, peer, and cultural influences.

Students cheat to get grades better than they think they would otherwise earn, of course. But why? Many students, and especially those with lower grade averages, say they cheat to survive; they do not think they can pass the course without resorting to dishonest means. By comparison, students with high grade averages say they cheat to get the best possible grades in order to gain a competitive advantage in the job market or in graduate school admission (Kibler 1993a; Kibler et al. 1995; McCabe and Pavela 1993). Barnett and Dalton (1981) concluded that "competition and pressure for good grades is unquestionably the single most important cause of academic dishonesty" (p. 549). Recent research at two small colleges reported by Graham, Monday, O'Brien, and Steffen (1994), suggests that many students today do not feel they have time to study and that while they may not have planned to cheat, they are open to the opportunity. In studying students' reactions to academic dishonesty, Jendrek (1992) found that, while 74 percent of her subjects had observed cheating, only 1 percent reported it to the instructor as required by university policy. She concluded, "students simply do not care about the cheating and feel indifferent to the offending student" (p. 271).

Much of the research on student characteristics is rather dated, and caution must be taken in applying it to today's students. Kibler (1993a) summarized much of it and concluded: (1) The majority of studies on student intelligence suggests that those less intelligent are more likely to cheat. But McCabe and Pavela (1993, p. 342) noted that "students at the top and the bottom of the grade point scale tend to engage in more academic dishonesty than the students in the middle." (2) Fraternity and sorority members are more likely to cheat, and closeness to others who cheat increases the likelihood of cheating. (3) Certain personality characteristics, such as extroversion, neuroticism, and anxiousness or tenseness, may be correlated with academic dishonesty. (4) Several other "behavioral characteristics"—actually an odd assortment of variables including self-sufficiency, ambitiousness, being severely punished by parents or not at all, not finding personal relevance in the course, etc.—have been studied and suggest that "differences do exist in the personal and behavioral characteristics" (Kibler 1993a, p. 257) of cheaters and non-cheaters.

Again, most of this research is rather old and may be of limited application to today's students, or of little help in understanding the dynamics of the phenomenon of cheating on contemporary campuses. Some recent research has sought to address attitudes of college students toward academic dishonesty as they are influenced by ethnicity and religious participation (Sutton and Huba 1995) and by gender, goal GPA, and student estimates of the frequency of cheating (Genereux and McLeod 1995). Roth and McCabe (1995) recently studied the relative importance of the values students bring with them to college, vis-a-vis specific communication strategies aimed at lessening cheating, and they found that the values of students are the stronger predictor.

Many institutional, peer, and cultural factors influencing academic dishonesty are cited in the literature. Gehring and Pavela summarized several:

- *Students are unaware of how academic dishonesty is defined. [Evidence in support of this was reported recently by Roth and McCabe (1995).]*
- *Student values have changed. The ability to succeed at all costs is one of the most cherished values. Students are more interested in financial security, power, and status and less committed to altruism, social concerns, and learning for the sake of learning.*
- *Increased competition for enrollment in popular disciplines and for admission to prestigious graduate and professional schools prompts students to cheat to improve their grades.*
- *Students believe that others cheat and get away with it, so they cheat, too.*
- *Cheating is not seen as deviant and is "neutralized" by excuses that have some basis in fact, such as the professor grades unfairly or was inaccessible, or "I can tell from the feedback that my papers are not read very carefully." "The professor doesn't care, so why should I?"*
- *The risks associated with cheating are minimal. Often faculty members avoid using campus disciplinary procedures and simply give a lower grade to students suspected of cheating. Where campus sanctions are imposed, they may not be appropriate for the severity of the infraction.*
- *Students are succumbing to frequent temptations. Faculty are careless about securing examinations, or proctoring exams, and frequently repeat the same assignments or examinations.*
- *Students do not believe, and are not challenged to understand that, what they are learning is relevant to their future careers* (1994, pp. 9-10).

Kibler (1993a) similarly noted that faculty members' teaching and evaluation styles and behaviors seem to be related to cheating, and that the faculty are an important element in the moral climate of the campus. Faculty members' attitudes toward cheating have been shown to have a significant effect on the extent to which academic honesty policies and processes are used and are effective (Jendrek 1989). McCabe and Pavela (1993) and McCabe and Trevino (1993) noted that schools with honor codes have significantly less cheating. May and Loyd's (1993) research findings support this conclusion. Genereux and McLeod (1995) found that only 19 percent of the variance on cheating is attributable to personal variables, and that some circumstances, especially pressure to get good grades and instructor indifference to cheating, "are apparently particularly important triggers for cheating" (p. 699). "[A] dramatic increase in student collaboration, where the professor had explicitly asked for individual work" (McCabe and Trevino 1996, p. 31), has been attributed to a lack of faculty clarity and consistency on the matter, resulting in students' confusion over what is acceptable collaboration on assignments.

In addition to studying the effect of honor codes (as noted above), McCabe and Trevino (1993) also studied the influence of other "contextual influences" on academic dishonesty, which they found to be more influential than the mere existence of an honor code. Based on their survey of 6,096 students from small and highly selective institutions, they determined that academic dishonesty is *inversely* related to the understanding and acceptance of academic integrity policies, to the perceived certainty of being reported by a peer, and to the perceived severity of penalties. They found academic dishonesty *positively* related to perceptions of peers' academic dishonesty. This last variable proved to be the most influential of all, leading them to suggest that:

> . . . *social learning theory may be particularly useful for understanding academic dishonesty behavior among college students. The strong influence of peers' behavior may suggest that academic dishonesty not only is learned from observing the behavior of peers, but that peers' behavior provides a kind of normative support for cheating. The fact that others are cheating may also suggest that, in such a climate, the non-cheater feels left at a disadvantage. Thus, cheating may come to be viewed as an acceptable way of getting and staying ahead* (McCabe and Trevino 1993, p. 533).

McCabe (in Kibler et al. 1995) labeled a campus climate characterized by widespread acceptance or tolerance of academic dishonesty as a "cheating culture."

Some broad, cultural/societal influences on students' values and ethics have been identified as contributing to the problem of academic dishonesty. The 1970s and 1980s have been characterized as the "me" decades, with "[i]ndividual ascendancy characterized by present orientation, hedonism,

Faculty members' attitudes toward cheating have been shown to have a significant effect on the extent to which academic honesty policies and processes are used and are effective.

a concern for personal rights, and duty to self . . ." (Gehring and Pavela 1994, p. 8). Astin's Cooperative Institutional Research Program has documented that students' motives for attending college became increasingly materialistic and decreasingly philosophic until recent years, during which there has been some resurgence of nonmaterialistic motives.

What Have Institutions of Higher Education Done to Address the Problem?

By far the single best source of information in answer to this question is provided by the research of William Kibler (1994). His research did not include two-year colleges and was limited to members of the Association for Student Judicial Affairs (ASJA), who may be better informed on the subject, more "professional" in their practice, and more judicial process-oriented than those who are not ASJA members (cf. Aaron 1992). The national survey of 300 public and private colleges and universities met with a good response rate (66 percent), especially from public institutions (84 percent), and it asked about many important policy and practice issues. He concluded:

1. *Disciplinary policies are prevalent and are the primary source guiding how institutions address academic dishonesty. The policies predominantly address it from a legal/due process perspective rather than a student development perspective. . . .*
2. *Honor codes are not prevalent as a source for guiding how institutions address academic dishonesty. Only one-fourth of the survey respondents indicated their institutions have an honor code. . . .*
3. *Systematic, comprehensive programs to promote academic integrity are not prevalent. . . .*
4. *The only prevalent methods of communicating about academic dishonesty are the traditional ones of student handbooks, catalogs, and new student orientation. . . . The failure of most institutions in the study to establish [an ethos promoting academic integrity] creates campus environments that foster cheating.*
5. *There is little involvement of students in developing and enforcing academic dishonesty policies or programs at most institutions. By failing to involve students in these processes, institutions foster an atmosphere of "us*

against them," which encourages cheating (Kibler 1994, pp. 100-101).

Prescriptions for Reducing Academic Dishonesty
The Center for Academic Integrity, a consortium of 85 institutions (McCabe and Trevino 1996) has recommended a number of strategies for improving academic integrity in students, including:

- *promoting student discussions of the value of academic integrity,*
- *informing students of the campus policies on academic integrity and involving them in the judicial process,*
- *encouraging faculty not to use the same exams consistently and urging them to discuss academic integrity in their classrooms.*

Using The University of Maryland's (College Park) Code of Academic Integrity as a model, Pavela and McCabe (1993) cited seven guiding principles for reducing academic dishonesty and reestablishing the value of academic integrity on college campuses:

1. *Develop clear, specific definitions of academic dishonesty and employ them uniformly in all parts of the institution.*
2. *Involve students in educating their peers about the importance of academic integrity, as well as in reporting and resolving academic dishonesty allegations.*
   Appeal to the students' sense of honor and personal integrity.
4. *Reduce the temptations to engage in academic dishonesty.*
5. *Encourage teaching styles and examinations that call for active student classroom participation and critical thinking rather than memorization.*
6. *Impose reasonable, but strict, penalties when academic dishonesty does occur.*
7. *Eliminate proceduralism in the resolution of academic dishonesty cases* (pp. 28-29).

Gehring and Pavela (1994) reviewed the literature on pedagogical strategies that faculty might use to improve teaching in ways that lessen the need, reasons, and opportunity for academic dishonesty. Their suggestions include advice about keeping all assignments relevant to course objectives, thus eliminating irrelevancy as a rationale for dishonesty; the importance of faculty knowing their students and their capabilities, thereby making students less inclined to substitute the work of others; communicating the institution's standards of academic integrity and reinforcing it in course syllabi, and testing and proctoring practices that make cheating harder.

The Need for Institutional Research

Before embarking on campaigns to reduce academic dishonesty, it is important for institutions to establish baseline data on it, both for the purpose of justifying expenditures and for program evaluation. Only six percent of Ludeman's (1988) respondents reported using campus research for this purpose. Although extrapolation from national studies, and collecting anecdotal/informal information from faculty, are no doubt useful to institutions as they approach the issue, "campus opinion polls and studies of academic integrity, and related issues, should be conducted on a regular basis to generate data that can be used to better assess the extent of the problem" (Ludeman 1988, p. 173).

Are Honor Codes the Answer?

Honor codes comprise a distinct subset of codes of conduct that speak primarily to academic matters. The first attempt at the creation of an honor code appears to have been as a part of the student government experiment at the University of Virginia in the 1800s. But it was during the early 1900s that the concept burgeoned, especially in the south. "By 1915, at least 123 American institutions of higher education were employing some variant of the honor system" (Brubacher and Rudy 1976, p. 125). Today, they are more common at small- and medium-sized private colleges, and although they seem to be a vestige of a time past, they have just recently been established at some institutions (Hoekema 1994).

Honor codes may be distinguished from other codes in three ways (Hoekema 1994). First, students are usually expected to explicitly agree to uphold an honor principle, sometimes including writing an "honor pledge" on all academic work submitted. Second, students usually have an inordinate part in the enforcement and revision of the code. On some campuses, professors routinely leave the room during examinations; the students themselves are expected to monitor behavior and attend to infractions. Third, students are expected to report any known violations by other students. This last feature, which is called "nontoleration" at the United States Air Force Academy (USAFA), is best illustrated by the crisp, nononsense language in USAFA's nontoleration clause that opens its honor code: "We will not lie, steal, cheat, nor tolerate among us anyone who does" (Roffey and Porter 1992).

There is evidence that honor codes "can be an effective component of efforts to promote and control academic honesty" (Pavela and McCabe 1993). Institutions with honor codes have less self-reported cheating, both in terms of the percentage of students who cheat and in the number of times students cheat, yet it should be obvious that they are not, in and of themselves, a panacea (Pavela 1993). Instead, they are probably not as influential as the social context factors that produce them or that result from the process of their establishment (McCabe and Trevino 1993). In this regard, the major points of a conference on academic integrity held at Rutgers University in 1992 are reiterated here:

There is evidence that honor codes "can be an effective component of efforts to promote and control academic honesty."

- *education must extend beyond the boundaries of the classroom and into questions of values and ethics,*
- *consideration of ethical issues must include all campus constituencies, especially students,*
- *communication between students, faculty members, and administrators about academic integrity must be open and risk-free, and there must be a sense of shared values or responsibility for academic integrity among students and faculty,*
- *honor codes are only part of the answer and will not work on every campus,*
- *a unique institutional character that is highly valued by students, faculty, and administrators alike is essential for promoting academic integrity,*
- *colleges and universities should concentrate on teaching values of integrity and honesty to their students rather than using resources only to police student dishonesty,*
- *the academic community must be supportive of students who choose to challenge academic dishonesty,*
- *although there is a place for punishment, the emphasis should be on counseling and rehabilitation for most students* (Pavela and McCabe 1993).

Pavela (1993) listed the disadvantages and advantages of honor codes. A careful consideration of his points may help institutions decide which, if any, features of honor codes they might attempt to implement on their campuses:

Disadvantages:

1. *Honor systems are seen by some students and faculty members as elitist and moralistic* (p. 354).
2. *Non-toleration clauses in the traditional honor codes are notoriously ineffective* (p. 354).
3. *Honor code schools relying on penalties like automatic expulsion often find that the fact-finding process in academic integrity hearings is distorted* (p. 354).
4. *Honor systems can be slow and cumbersome* (p. 354).
5. *Honor systems require constant attention* (p. 355). *They are labor intensive.*
6. *A student-run honor system is a learning experience for the individuals involved* (p. 355). *The quality of hearings and reports may be uneven.*
7. *Finally, honor systems are a magnet for controversy. . . . [C]ampus administrators with a low tolerance for contention and disagreement will find student-run honor systems unappealing* (p. 355).

Advantages:

1. *Academic dishonesty is more likely to occur in a campus environment where the student peer group condones or even encourages it. Honor codes influence the peer culture and encourage students to affirm to other students the importance of academic integrity* (p. 355).
2. *Honor systems promote moral discourse on campus, especially within the student peer group and they normally generate frequent discussions about ethical values, and the proper role of rules and sanctions* (p. 355).
3. *Honor codes affirm basic human values and personal virtues, like diligence, patience, self-discipline, a willingness to consider alternative hypotheses, and honesty, even across cultural differences* (p. 367).
4. *Honor systems foster the role modeling of students actively involved in them.*
5. *Honor systems positively impact the character formation of those who serve in them.*

6. *Honor systems thrive on maintaining and creating [positive] traditions* (p. 368).
7. *Honor systems also tell students they are valued, and can be entrusted with the responsibility for helping to mold some of the most important aspects of campus culture* (p. 368).
8. *Entrusting students with maintaining institutional standards increases the likelihood those standards will be seen as legitimate by the student body as a whole (368).*
9. *Finally, honor systems merit consideration because many of them seem to work* (p. 368).

Pavela concluded:

> *Finally, in the midst of all the difficulties associated with making an honor code work, you may find that even the skeptics have come to the conclusion that some kind of honor code is the best of many imperfect ways to promote and protect academic integrity. That's our conclusion as well. To the question is it a new day for honor codes?" our answer is a qualified yes* (1993, p. 369).

Summary

Academic dishonesty (cheating on tests, plagiarism, and other forms of taking unfair advantage in coursework) is an old and widespread problem that is of continuing concern. Today's students, faced with a future in a stagnant economy and disenchanted with the perceived lack of integrity in the greater society, may be succumbing to increased pressure to cheat, and their cheating may be taking new forms made easier by computer technology.

College and university officials are encouraged to develop broad-based strategies to promote an ethos of academic integrity and to combat the "cheating culture." Faculty should be trained to employ testing procedures that render cheating difficult, while students should be taught the importance of academic honesty. Students and faculty must be engaged in policy formulation and the adjudication of academic misconduct. Honor codes appear to have value in this regard, insofar as they stimulate a climate of dialogue about the purposes of academy and reinforce the value of academic integrity.

CODES OF CONDUCT: LEGAL ISSUES AND EDUCATIONAL CONSIDERATIONS

Codes of conduct is written guidance for colleges and universities of what constitutes acceptable behavior on the campus and related to the institution's mission. They typically contain three elements: the rules of conduct themselves, the procedures that are to be followed when a code violation is alleged, and the possible sanctions that may be applied if a violation is determined.

In the colonial colleges, lengthy and detailed lists of both proscribed and prescribed behaviors dictated the students daily living, with the intent of molding their spiritual and moral character. Colleges had both legal and educational warrant to control their young charge though their charters, through the support and involvement of lay overseers, through community and parental expectation, and by the disinclination of the courts to meddle in the work of the academy.

In recent times, the courts have continued to give deference to colleges and universities in "academic" matters (e.g., grading, tenure), while they have been much less likely to defer to the academy's expertise in matters of procedure, which are often viewed through the lens of the contract theory. Both public and private institutions have been held accountable by the courts for following their own rules; however, the reach of the rules of conduct—a matter of substantive due process—may be different for public and private schools.

The Public-Private Dichotomy
The law often treats public and private institutions differently, and these differences are critical to understanding the law's impact on the scope of colleges' codes of conduct. Today's public institutions of higher learning in the United States are prevented by the Fourteenth Amendment from engaging in activity that violates the federal Constitution (Kaplin and Lee 1995). Yet, they may still establish and enforce codes of conduct so long as they do not violate one or more of the following well-established principles of substantive due process:

- *They may make and enforce rules of student conduct to foster discipline and maintain order.*
- *Behavioral standards, including those applied to off-campus behavior, must be consistent with the institution's lawful purpose and function.*

- *Rules must be specific enough to give adequate notice of expected behaviors and to allow the preparation of a defense against a charge under them. Vague or overly broad rules have not been upheld.*
- *The code of conduct should be written and available to all.*
- *Rules cannot be applied in a discriminatory manner.*
- *Rules must be constitutionally fair, reasonable, and not capricious or arbitrary.*
- *The constitutionally guaranteed rights of students can be limited to enable the institution to function, but blanket prohibitions or restraints are not permitted.*
- *Students' First Amendment rights of freedom of assembly and expression may not be limited, except for compelling reasons, such as for the protection of someone's safety.*
- *Students are protected from unreasonable searches and seizures by the Fourth Amendment. Residence hall rooms may not be entered and examined, except to further the educational aims of the institution, which includes protection of its facilities* (Buchanan 1978; Correnti 1988; Gehring and Bracewell 1992; Gibbs 1992; Pavela 1985).

Private institutions, insofar as they are not engaged in "state action," and therefore, do not fall under the Fourteenth Amendment, are not required by the Constitution to follow these principles—their relationship with their students is viewed by the law as largely contractual—and, hence, they have more lattitude in making disciplinary rules. Yet, as Kaplin and Lee have suggested, "the principles [of substantive due process] reflect basic notions of fairness, which can be critical components of good administrative practice; thus, administrators of private institutions may wish to use them as policy guides in formulating their codes" (1995, p. 459). In fact, because reforms tend to become normative in American higher education, many private colleges and universities now contract with their students to provide basic due process protections, and having done so, they are contractually bound to follow their own rules (Kaplin and Lee 1995; Pavela 1985; Shur 1988).

Principles for Drafting a Code of Conduct
Stoner and Cerminara (1990) offered four principles that should be kept in mind when drafting a student disciplinary

code: (1) It should "follow the general dictates of due process." (2) It "need not be drafted with the specificity of criminal statutes;" it "should avoid language implying that criminal standards apply;" but it should "be sufficiently specific to make the rules clear." (3) Any model student conduct code, such as the one they offered in their article [see Appendix A], only represents the generally prevailing law and should be reviewed by the institution's legal counsel to ensure that it fits local case law. (4) A code should do more than prohibit behaviors; it should recognize students' rights, thereby assuring students that the institution does not intend to take away rights, "but merely intends to control action going beyond the exercise of such rights." The authors suggested that such a statement be included in a preamble to the student code or in the student handbook (pp. 92-93).

In crafting codes of conduct, institutions should avoid the related problems of vagueness and overbreadth (such as a proscription against "misconduct"), while also resisting the temptation to try to list all possible infractions. Footer (1996) has suggested a framework for the inevitable list of prohibited behaviors which is comprised of four broad catagories: Violations against the college and university community, violations against property, violations against persons, and violations against federal, state, or local laws. Further, she recommends that, besides filling out these catagories with more specific prohibitions, examples should be used to illuminate the intention of the code's provisions (pp. 21-22) .

Research on Codes of Conduct
The published research on codes of student conduct is quite limited and may be simply divided into two categories, one comprised of two studies (Dannells 1990; Lancaster, Cooper and Harman 1993) about the extent to which students are informed about the rules (a basic element of substantive due process), and one qualitative look at what kinds of behaviors are proscribed (Hoekema 1994).

The research on the extent to which students are informed of the codes of conduct suggests that while the majority of colleges and universities publish or make their student conduct rules available, a significant minority—probably somewhere between 15 percent and 25 percent—do not adequately inform students of their rules. This "oversight" might be the basis for a student's defense or later legal appeal, that he or she was not given sufficient notice of the standard of behavior and could not reasonably comply.

Hoekema's (1994) study of college codes of conduct included a content analysis of documents provided to him by a group of "leading institutions," admittedly a nonrandom sample because of the over-representation of liberal arts and selective institutions. Nonetheless, his findings are of interest, especially if one accepts his premise that other institutions are more likely to borrow policy ideas from schools in his sample than the reverse:

> *If all one knew of student behavior came from student handbooks and disciplinary codes, one's impression of the life of the contemporary college student would be bizarre. Certainly one would not mistake today's campus for the restrictive and moralistic domain of a benevolent dean acting in loco parentis. Today, the handbooks seem to imply, the problems of sexual exploitation and drug abuse pale to insignificance in comparison with the threat posed by extension cords* (p. 66).

His flippancy about the very real fire hazard of improperly used electrical cords in residence halls notwithstanding, Hoekema's point is an engaging one. He found comparatively little emphasis on such moral and social issues as cohabitation, alcohol and other drug abuse, and sexual exploitation, which he interpreted as either ambivalence or permissiveness. Only in the areas of academic dishonesty and procedural due process protections did he find campus rules, in general, to be unequivocal and unambiguous.

Codes of Conduct and the Special Problem of Hate Speech

Although hate speech prohibitions at public institutions have been struck down in the courts on First Amendment grounds, some institutions persist in enacting rules that would regulate certain kinds of expression aimed at harassing or abusing members of minority groups (Shea 1995). "Hate speech" has been defined as:

> *an imprecise, catch-all term that generally includes verbal and written words and symbolic acts that con-*

vey a grossly negative assessment of particular persons or groups based on their race, gender, ethnicity, religion, sexual orientation, or disability. Hate speech thus is highly derogatory and degrading, and the language is typically coarse. The purpose of the speech is more to humiliate or wound than it is to communicate ideas or information (Kaplin and Lee 1995, p. 509).

A thorough treatment of the legal aspects of this complex and heated issue is well beyond the scope of this work. [For an excellent review of the case law on hate speech, the reader is directed to Kaplin and Lee (1995, pp. 508-516)]. Nonetheless, Kaplin and Lee have enumerated "five major free speech principles" that should be considered by any public institution undertaking to proscribe students' speech or expression:

1. *Regulations on the content of speech—that is, the speaker's message—are highly suspect.*
2. *The emotional content, as well as the cognitive content is protected from government regulation.*
3. *Speech may not be prohibited merely because persons, who hear [it] or view it, are offended by the message.*
4. *Government may not regulate speech activity with provisions whose language is either overly broad or vague and would thereby create a chilling effect on the exercise of free speech rights.*
5. *When government is regulating what is considered an unprotected type of speech—for example, fighting words, or obscenity—it generally may not restrict expression of other topics and viewpoints within that same area* (pp. 513-514).

Kaplin and Lee continue, "[i]n light of the imposing barriers to regulation erected by these principles, it is critical that institutions (public and private) emphasize *nonregulatory* approaches for dealing with hate speech" (p. 514).

For those institutions that decide to regulate speech itself, Kaplan and Lee offer six potential types of regulations that may not violate one of the preceding five principles:

1. *When hate speech is combined with nonspeech actions in the same course of behavior, institutions may regulate*

Kaplin and Lee have enumerated "five major free speech principles" that should be considered by any public institution undertaking to proscribe students' speech or expression.

the nonspeech elements of behavior without violating the First Amendment.

2. Institutions may regulate the time and place at which hate speech is uttered, or the manner in which it is uttered, as long as they use neutral regulations that do not focus on the content or viewpoint of the speech.

3. Institutions may regulate the content of hate speech that falls within one of the various exceptions to the principle forbidding content-based restrictions on speech. For example, "fighting words"—"words that by their very utterance tend to incite an immediate breach of the peace"—may be prohibited (UMW Post, cited in Gibbs 1992, p. 13).

4. Institutions probably may regulate hate speech in the forms of threats or intimidation aimed at particular individuals and creating in them a realistic fear for their physical safety or the security of their property.

5. Institutions probably may regulate hate speech that occurs on, or is projected onto private areas, such as dormitory rooms or library study carrels, and thereby infringes on privacy interests of individuals who legitimately occupy these places.

6. Institutions probably may regulate hate speech that furthers a scheme of racial or other discrimination (pp. 514-515).

The use of the qualifying word "probably" in the last three examples above should serve as a reminder that this area of the law, perhaps more than most, is still evolving. Campus decision-makers contemplating the formulation of a hate speech code, would be wise to confer with legal counsel before proceeding.

In looking for a rationale to *not* formulate such a prohibition, one would be hard-pressed to find a more eloquent expression of the civil libertarian position of Yale University's formal statement of why it has no such policy:

We take a chance, as the First Amendment takes a chance, when we commit ourselves to the idea that the results of free expression are to the general benefit in the long run, however unpleasant they may appear at the time. The validity of such a belief cannot be demonstrated conclusively. It is a belief of recent historical

development, even within universities, one embodied in
American constitutional doctrine, but not widely
shared outside the academic world, and denied in
theory, and in practice, by much of the world, most of
the time. . . .

No member of the university with a decent respect for
others should use, or encourage others to use, slurs and
epithets intended to discredit another's race, ethnic
group, religion, or sex. It may sometimes be necessary
in a university for civility and mutual respect to be
superseded by the need to guarantee free expression
(Hoekema 1994, p. 107).

Summary

Codes of student conduct, typically found in catalogs or
student handbooks, are higher education institutions' way of
informing students about the values of the academy as they
affect the limits of student behavior and about the consequences of violating those limits. Most colleges and universities inform students through provision of a written form of
the code, although a significant minority do not. Codes must
be carefully drafted, both legally and educationally within
the scope of the educational mission of the individual institution. Broad and vague proscriptions of behavior are generally not legal, and similarly, overly broad prescriptions are of
dubious educational value. The issue of hate speech is particularly problematic, because it resides at the interface of
constitutional liberties and the humanistic values of tolerance and open-mindedness that are so fundamental to
American higher education.

HOEKEMA'S MODEL OF STUDENT DISCIPLINE

David Hoekema, a professor of philosophy and academic dean at Calvin College in Grand Rapids, Michigan, undertook an extensive study of college disciplinary programs as part of the series "Issues in Academic Ethics" (1994), edited by Steven M. Cahn. From the unique viewpoint of an ethicist, Hoekema studied the history of student discipline and present day campus rules and judicial mechanisms. He engaged in both a survey of administrators and a careful content analysis of codes of student conduct, gathered from prestigious and selective colleges and universities. He found a vacuum, left by the demise of *in loco parentis,* that is partially and insufficiently filled by detailed rules of adjudicatory processes, as well as vague and lofty goals that provide no basis for measuring success or failure. He argued that:

> *[e]ven though rules and procedures must reflect local circumstances, the rules may still serve many of the same ends. . . . [S]uch a common ground does exist, and the . . . overall goals can be articulated in a way that is broad enough to transcend different implementations but specific enough to offer a basis for assessing success* (Hoekema 1994, p. 118).

He proposed three distinct, overarching goals that systems of campus discipline seek, or *should* seek, to achieve: 1) To prevent exploitation and harm to students; 2) To promote an atmosphere conducive to free discussion and learning; and 3) To nurture a sense of mutual responsibility and moral community in students. These goals—"each of them firmly rooted in basic moral ideals" (p. 136)—"constitute a summary of the legitimate purposes of student conduct regulation. . . . We should be able to classify a particular rule, policy, or procedure as serving [one or more of them]" (p. 134).

Hoekema illustrated how these goals may be used in a classificatory scheme and an analytic framework to identify reasons for existing rules and assessing proposed rules with the following table:

Purposes of Specific Areas of Discipline

Policy area	1. To prevent harm	2. To uphold freedom	3. To foster community
Plagiarism	■	■	■
Alcohol abuse	■		■
Drug use	■		■
Sexual mores			■
Rape	■		■
Abusive speech	■	■	■

Hoekema (1994) further proposed that: "[w]ith respect to any particular category of undesirable behavior, there are essentially three stances that an institution may adopt" (p. 139): 1) a restrictive stance, for those areas where the institution decides strict regulation is warranted; 2) a permissive stance, for those areas where the institution wishes to emphasize students' responsibility to make their own moral decisions and where the institution is unable to make decisions for them; and 3) a directive stance, where neither of the former approaches apply and where the institution seeks to influence student behavior in ways other than by rules and sanctions, such as by example or persuasion.

Hoekema's model also includes a way of considering what behaviors are appropriate for disciplinary control. He suggested:

[i]n the clearest cases . . . three distinct conditions hold and together provide a basis for the institution's effort at control. They are:

1. *The prohibited conduct is unacceptable on campus.*
2. *The prohibited conduct can be effectively prevented or deterred.*

*3. Reliable and fair measures of enforcement are available
to the institution* (p. 146).

By correlating the three stances an institution may take
toward disapproved behavior with the three conditions that
characterize behavior appropriate for discipline, the institution can more systematically determine its approach to various areas of student conduct. Hoekema (1994) depicted this
set of correlations by the following table:

Conditions for the Three Disciplinary Approaches

	Appropriateness of policy stance		
Which conditions hold?	Restrictive	Directive	Permissive
1, 2, and 3	Yes	[Yes]	[Yes]
1 and 2 only	No	Yes	[Yes]
1 only	No	No	Yes

*Cells marked [Yes] indicate that,
although the stance indicated may be appropriate,
it is unlikely to be used as more forceful means are also available.*

Hoekema acknowledged the difficulty of categorizing conduct in certain areas, especially hate speech and exploitive
sexual behavior, and argued convincingly that most institutions need a directive stance "by which the institution can
communicate both to its members and to the world outside
the inappropriateness of the behavior in question. It can
guide students away from such abuses without legislating
against them" (p. 156). In answer to his question—"How is it
possible to convey institutional disapprobation without the
formal structure of rules and sanctions?" (p. 156)—Hoekema
recommended "three steps toward moral community":

*1. [A]n institution's principal administrators should acknow-
ledge the importance of the values that are under threat
and the seriousness of the offenses that threaten them.*

2. *[A]dministrators and members of the faculty should engage students actively and creatively in an effort to resolve the problem.*

3. *[I]n cases in which the promulgation of rules and enforcement of sanctions is ill-advised and ineffective, institutions should seek instead to shape behavior by identifying positive models in the campus community* (p. 157).

Lastly, Hoekema emphasized the centrality of community in any effort to foster moral development and the power of modeling in the process, and he reminded us that:

> *. . . to rely on ever more strenuous enforcement of disciplinary rules and codes is an inherently ill-suited tactic, if one's goal is to assist students to become mature and responsible moral agents. Institutions ought rather to devote their efforts to systematic encouragement of the small communities contained on campus, in which moral reflection and thoughtful choice flourish* (p. 159).

Hoekema closed his book by relating the idea of community with the overarching goal of student discipline:

> *To form a genuine community, by fostering and encouraging the numerous smaller communities, in which students and faculty find their place and form their identity, is the ultimate goal of the entire system of student conduct regulation and discipline* (p. 166).

The centrality of the idea of community building is a broad-based approach to addressing disciplinary affairs that finds support in the literature on student integration (Tinto 1993) and student involvement (Astin 1985, 1993). What is often lacking in students who act out in violation of campus rules, is a sense of belonging and of being a valued member of the campus community. If it is true that "[s]tudents' academic and social integration affects positively their persistence on campus" (Gardiner 1994), then it stands to reason that the same integration would positively affect student behavior while on the campus. Furthermore, it may be that a pervasive sense of alienation and the decline in students' sense of psychological well-being is related to the degree of support they feel in their college environment (Gardiner 1994).

Summary

Hoekema's model of student discipline is unique in that it focuses from a perspective of moral and educational philosophy, rather than the legalistic view that has dominated so much of the thinking about student discipline in recent years. It is a useful model that includes overarching, ethical goals for discipline, general strategies or "stances" that institutions may adopt, and a way of considering what behaviors are appropriate for disciplinary control. He emphasized the importance of developing a moral community (and smaller sub-communities) on the campus, the power of modeling in the process, and the role dialogue plays in it. Those seeking to consider anew their campus' disciplinary approach would find ample fuel in Hoekema's ideas for thought and discussion.

The centrality of the idea of community building is a broad-based approach to addressing disciplinary affairs that finds support in the literature on student integration.

THE ORGANIZATION AND ADMINISTRATION OF CAMPUS DISCIPLINARY/JUDICIAL SYSTEMS

The Nature and Scope of Campus Discipline/Judicial Systems

Where once the fatherly president, with the support and active involvement of the faculty, and later the dean, handled discipline in an informal and individualistic way, discipline today involves definite organizational structures and processes. As Smith (1994) pointed out, "[d]isciplinary systems today, for the most part, are indeed systems. They have a process for enforcing regulations and different, distinct roles for individuals and committees to play" (p. 84).

The research on campus disciplinary/judicial systems is consistent in one important respect: From institution to institution there is substantial heterogeneity in approaches to student discipline (Dannells 1978, 1990; Durst 1969; Dutton, Smith and Zarle 1969; Lancaster et al. 1993; Ostroth and Hill 1978; Steele, Johnson and Rickard 1984). The nature of these campus systems will vary depending on such institutional factors as history, tradition, locale, philosophy/mission, size, type of control (public or private), residential character, the needs of the community, and the extent to which governance is shared with students (Ardaiolo and Walker 1987, Hoekema 1994; Lancaster et al. 1993).

Campus disciplinary systems vary in nature and scope on several key dimensions:

- *Scope of the code of conduct—How does the institution define the extent of its authority and responsibility, or, in the legal term, its jurisdiction? How specifically is behavior defined and proscribed? Does it speak to violations of the criminal law? Does it distinguish between academic and nonacademic (social) misconduct?*
- *Nature of the process—How formal, complex, or legalistic is it? What choices or alternatives do students have between different adjudicative mechanisms? What due process rights are accorded the student, both before and during the hearing phase of the process? What appeals are available? What sanctions/actions are available? Which sanctions/actions are most used?*
- *Student Involvement—What are the nature and extent of student input into the code of conduct? What is the level of student involvement in the process of adjudication? To what extent are students involved in the actual management of the system and the maintenance of records?*

- *Where does discipline fit into the administration of the institution?*

Who Is Responsible for Discipline?

With few exceptions, student discipline today is the province of student personnel (or student affairs) administrators (Lancaster et al. 1993) who are delegated the responsibility by the president, bringing a range of styles to the task (Appleton et al. 1978), and whose roles may be viewed on a spectrum. At one end of the spectrum, they may function as an ombudsman or mediator, independently and informally facilitating the resolution of conflicts and dealing with minor complaints. The advantages of this approach include brevity, keeping the problem at the lowest/closest level of resolution, and providing a nonadversarial alternative for settling differences in certain settings (Hayes and Balogh 1990; Serr and Taber 1987; Sisson and Todd 1995). At the other end of the spectrum, there may be a specialist, charged with the responsibility of a more formal, legalistic disciplinary system, including managing the operation of one or more hearing boards, handling disciplinary records, and investigating and preparing cases in more serious matters. This model has the advantages of specialization: expertise and freeing others from discipline. Continuity, equity, and improved management may also result from such specialization (Steele et al. 1984).

Judicial affairs specialists are uncommon in smaller schools; they are more likely to be found in large, public, and commuter institutions. At smaller and private institutions, the dean of students is most likely the person with the major responsibility for adjudicating student misconduct. The most common model is that of a mid-level student affairs professional, usually associated with the dean of students office or with the office of residence life (housing), who handles minor violations, while preparing and presenting more serious cases—especially those that might result in dismissal—to a hearing board for a final recommendation or disposition (Dannells 1978, 1990; Lancaster et al. 1993; Ostroth, Armstrong and Campbell 1978; Steele et al. 1984).

The Basic Functions of the Disciplinary Specialist

In their day-to-day activities, student personnel administrators, who are charged primarily with disciplinary affairs, perform many routine administrative duties. At a much broader level, Caruso (1978) defined the important roles of the student discipline specialist in terms of the basic student personnel functions outlined by Miller and Prince:

- **Goal-setting** *keeps the discipline system in concert with broader institutional goals, keeps the development of students to the fore, and is useful in designing outcome-oriented training programs for student judicial boards.*
- **Assessing student growth** *provides important, but commonly lacking, data about the efficacy of the disciplinary program for all of the students involved.*
- **Instruction**, *such as that involved in student leadership training and judicial board member education, contributes to the effectiveness of the disciplinary process.*
- **Consultation** *includes working with the campus disciplinary policy/rules committee, judicial boards, and staff members in residence halls, as well as assisting academic units with the administration of academic misconduct cases.*
- **Environmental management** *involves any response to a behavior problem that is intended to reduce or eliminate conditions that contribute to the problem, such as making changes in the placement of residence hall fire safety equipment, in campus lighting, or in policies regarding sale or use of alcohol on campus.*
- **Program evaluation** *describes the important function through which the discipline program studies itself for purposes of improvement and justification of resources and is closely related to goal setting and assessment (1976).*

Another function, basic to the educational approach to discipline, is *disciplinary counseling*, which Williamson (1963) defined as "sympathetic but firm counseling to aid the individual to gain insight and be willing to accept restrictions on his [or her] individual autonomy and behavior" (p. 13). Other frequently cited objectives of disciplinary counseling include behavior change, insight, maturation, emotional stability, moral judgment, self-reliance, self-control, and understanding and accepting responsibility for consequences of personal behavior. The counseling techniques of "information-giving" (teaching) and confrontation are central to this kind of encounter and may be employed throughout the disciplinary process (Ostroth and Hill 1978).

Research on Trends in the Administration of Student Discipline

For some 30 years, the administration of student discipline, and particularly the provision of due process safeguards, has been the focus of at least eight separate studies (Dannells 1978, 1990; Durst 1969; Dutton et al. 1969; Leslie and Satryb 1974; Ostroth et al. 1978; Steele et al. 1984; Van Alstyne 1963). Based on that research, the following trends are noted:

- In the 1960s, there was a dramatic increase in student input into rules, procedures, and the adjudication of misconduct. Student involvement remains high on most campuses today.
- In the decade following the *Dixon v. Alabama State Board of Education* (1961) decision, there was a similar trend in the provision of both procedural and substantive due process mechanisms, starting with a big shift toward more legalistic processes, but leveling in recent years. Today, on almost all campuses, students can expect to be afforded notice and a hearing when charged with a serious offense that might result in dismissal. The more serious the charge, the more formal and legalistic the process. Minor cases are commonly handled less formally.
- Milder sanctions are employed more often than stiffer penalties. Warnings, both oral and written, and disciplinary probation have been, and continue to be, the most common responses to student misconduct.
- Disciplinary counseling continues to be the most frequently used rehabilitative or reeducative action, but over the years, it is increasingly more likely to take place in either a disciplinary specialist's office or in the counseling center, especially in larger universities. At smaller schools, the entire disciplinary function, including post-hearing counseling, continues to be done in the dean of student's office.
- Most institutions do not anticipate changes in their programs/systems, but some have indicated a need for simpler, less legalistic processes.
- From campus to campus, diversity continues to characterize the administration of disciplinary affairs.

Models for the Professional Practice of Disciplinary Affairs and Judicial Programs

Two models for the practice of disciplinary affairs and judicial programs are to be found. The Council for the Advancement of

Standards for Student Services/Developmental Programs' *Standards and Guidelines for Judicial Programs and Services* (CAS 1988) includes general guidance about the mission and objectives of such programs, the organization and administration of them, training of judicial body members, human resources, ethics, and program evaluation. The Association for Student Judicial Affairs' *Statement of Ethical Principles and Standards of Conduct* (ASJA 1993; see Appendix B) is focused more on the ethics, behavior, and supervision of professionals who administer standards of student conduct, yet it also includes general guidance on development of campus rules and procedures.

Drawing upon the CAS Standards, the ASJA Statement, and the research base on the subject, note the following process model for organizing and administering the disciplinary function:

1. *Assign, as a primary responsibility, all disciplinary administration to a single staff member, even where multiple hearing bodies exist.*
2. *Place this staff member in a direct reporting relationship to the president or chief student affairs officer.*
3. *Create a philosophy for this staff member's practice and for the disciplinary system that fosters a developmental approach to discipline.*
4. *Create a formal training and assessment procedure, supported by appropriate documentation, for judicial officers and other regular participants* (Lancaster et al. 1993, p. 118).

Disciplinary Hearing Boards

Disciplinary hearing boards, or judicial tribunals, are a common feature in most campus systems. At larger institutions and on residential campuses, more than one board may exist, and they may be parallel in responsibility or they may be hierarchical. On a residential campus, for example, each hall may have its own hearing panel and another board may exist for inter-hall problems or for appeals from the individual hall boards. Another possibility is that a campus may have one hearing panel for academic dishonesty proceedings and another for nonacademic or social misconduct. Many campuses have one tribunal that hears all "serious" cases, i.e., those that might result in loss of credit, as in the case of academic dishonesty, or in dismissal, for any reason.

The composition of hearing boards varies, as does the research on them. Dannells (1978, 1990) found that a combination of students and faculty and/or staff is by far the most common composition and that the composition of hearing boards changed little, from 1977 to 1987. By comparison, Hoekema (1994) found administrators-only committees to be the most common composition; however, his item was worded "Administrators only (or an administrator)," which would include the "informal" process of a single hearing officer often used in minor cases on most campuses (p. 64, Table 3-4).

The selection and training of students for service on judicial boards are important processes that occupy much of the time of the campus hearing officer (or judicial advisor), whether he or she is a faculty member, a student affairs generalist, or a disciplinary/judicial specialist. Their importance is materially illustrated by the 113-page *Model Judicial Board Selection and Training Manual* published by the Commission on Campus Judicial Affairs and Legal Issues of the American College Personnel Association (ACPA 1993). The manual's statement of philosophy, adapted from UCLA's training manual, contains the essence of the primary benefit of using judicial boards:

> *The unique advantage of a student judicial board lies in the opportunity for students to influence the attitudes and subsequent behavior of other students through a formally constituted judicial mechanism. Without question, peer influence, exercised through the disciplinary process, can often be more effective in redirecting the behavior patterns of students than any other method of discipline within the institution* (p. 3).

A secondary benefit to the inclusion of students on hearing boards is the education of the student board members themselves. The process of peer review is an exercise in democratic living and community responsibility, and should no doubt affect the board member in positive, developmental ways. Even if the student is not selected to serve, the selection process alone may be of benefit for he/she may be exposed to thought-provoking interview questions like these excerpted from the "Suggested Questions for Individual Interviews" section of the ACPA manual:

- *Why do you want to be involved with the Judicial Board?*
- *What do you see as the purpose of the Judicial Board? Educative vs. Punitive? Where do they overlap?*
- *What are some of your strengths? How will these contribute to the board?*
- *How important do you think first impressions are to you? How do you compensate for your initial impression of someone?*
- *When should a student be punished for a policy violation?*
- *If you could rewrite our student regulations, what would you delete? What would you add?* (p. 10).

Both the selection and training sections of the manual include structured group activities and student conduct dilemmas, in which participation would likely be beneficial to candidates and/or board members. The remainder of the manual is devoted to examples of definitional responsibility for various board members, procedures and forms, and suggestions for using developmental theory to insure fairness, as well as for sanctioning. For someone starting or revamping a campus judicial system with student involvement, this selection and training manual would be a valuable resource.

Sanctions and Other Responses to Student Misconduct
Once a student has been judged to have violated a rule of an institution's code of conduct, the institutional response will generally fall in one of three categories: punitive (commonly called "sanctions"), rehabilitative (educational and developmental are more popular terms today), and environmental (actions directed at external causes). Of course, the extent to which a particular sanction is punitive, as opposed to developmental, is a matter relating to point of view and purpose. Frederickson (1992) argued that sanctions are a proper and effective therapeutic intervention for impulsive college students. Similarly, Pavela (1985) has provided a rationale for "just punishment" as a tool in fostering moral development in college students.

The sanctions that are most commonly used include:

- "informative" disciplinary communications, such as oral and written warnings, which are often accompanied by reference to more severe sanctions should the problem continue

A secondary benefit to the inclusion of students on hearing boards is the education of the student board members themselves.

- disciplinary probation
- loss of privileges or liberties, such as restrictions on social hours or the use of facilities, sometimes as a condition of probation
- restitution or compensation for damage or injury
- required service or labor
- fines
- denial of financial assistance, now thought to be rare, although the loss of an athletic scholarship would have the same effect
- actions that affect the student's status with the institution, such as suspension for either a finite or indefinite period, or expulsion (permanent dismissal).

Although, in recent years, some campuses have added to the range of their available sanctions by adding fines and required service/labor, the actual use of disciplinary sanctions and rehabilitative actions has changed little (Dannells 1991).

Rehabilitative, educational, or developmental responses to student misconduct commonly include counseling, referral to an educational program (e.g., alcohol/drug education), referral to medical or psychiatric services, and the assignment of service work intended to heighten the individual's sense of personal responsibility. Disciplinary counseling may be done by a professional counselor, by an administrator or faculty member involved with the disciplinary program, by someone outside the institution, such as a clergy person, a social worker, or other helping professional. The challenge of developmental discipline is addressed in another section of this report.

Environmentally-targeted responses that are intended to remove or reduce external causes of misconduct might include changing the student's living conditions, finding financial assistance, or work. Academic misbehavior that results from poor academic preparation might be addressed through tutoring or study skills development. Lastly, policy or program revision may be necessary where the misconduct is a function of antiquated or unnecessarily restrictive rules, where undesirable behavior (e.g., alcohol abuse) is fostered by an event that has become untenable or disruptive.

The institutional response in a disciplinary situation may be affected by several considerations, including the institution's educational mission and disciplinary philosophy as reflected in its behavioral standards and processes, the degree of divergence or congruence between those standards and the student culture, the behavior itself, the individual's background and the kinds of information that are to be considered (Janosik 1995), the range and flexibility of available responses, and the creativity of the decision-maker(s). On this last point, the reader might find useful Phelps and Burchell's *A Guide to Creative Sanctions.*

Janosik (1995) studied judicial decision-making and sanctioning and compared his findings with two studies conducted 30 years earlier. He found a consensus between groups of faculty, students, and administrators that a student's statement and previous record were the most important information in judicial decision-making and that this finding was consistent with Sillers and Feder's (1964). He also found agreement between those three groups on their views of the seriousness of certain violations. Assaults of all types, sale of illicit drugs, and grand theft were viewed as "extremely serious violations." Comparing his findings with those of Hodinko (1964), he noted that planning a demonstration and sexual promiscuity, which were viewed as serious problems 30 years earlier, did not make the top 10 most serious for either faculty or administrators in 1994. Furthermore, he noted that illegal use or abuse of alcohol were not viewed as serious violations in his or Hodinko's study.

Janosik's study is of interest on two other points. One is that "counseling records" were in his list of source information, and they were ranked as relatively important by all three groups. Should these not be strictly confidential and unavailable to judicial decision-makers? Secondly, Janosik's study, since it asked "what types of sanctions should be attached to selected acts of student misconduct?" is based on the premise that the sanction should fit the offense, rather than the offender, and is reflective of the "crime and punishment" view of student discipline.

Summary
Student discipline today, at virtually every college and university, is a system with rules, a process for the enforcement of those rules, and distinct roles for various individuals and committees. From campus to campus, these systems vary according to the size, type, and mission of the institution on such dimensions as the scope of the code of conduct, the level of formality and complexity of the process, the degree

of student involvement, and where discipline fits into the administration of the school.

At small colleges, the chief student affairs officer (CSAO) is likely to retain an active role in discipline, while at larger colleges and universities he/she is more likely to delegate the day-to-day administration of discipline to a mid-level specialist who handles minor complaints, and shares major ones, with the CSAO and the appropriate hearing board.

The research on trends in the administration of student discipline over the last 30 years shows a rush to institute due process protections following the *Dixon* case in 1961 and a preoccupation with proceduralism that lasted into the 1980s. Schools that foresee changes in their approach to discipline hope to develop simpler, less "legalistic" processes. Student rights, in the adjudication of misconduct and in the management of disciplinary records, are generally well protected, and student involvement in campus judicial systems is high. This student involvement, especially on hearing boards, which are a common feature of campus judicial systems, raises the issue of how to keep disciplinary records confidential. Training of student board members in this regard is essential, and it may be prudent for the protection of the institution to obtain a signed release from the accused before proceeding with an "open" hearing.

Both the Council for the Advancement of Standards (CAS) and the Association for Student Judicial Affairs (ASJA) have promulgated standards for the practice of disciplinary affairs and judicial programs. A simple process model for organizing and administering the disciplinary function is also available.

A variety of institutional responses, both punitive and educational, to student misconduct are available. Over time, the frequency of use for the most common disciplinary sanctions/responses has changed little, although there seems to have been an increase in referrals and/or requirements for counseling.

KEY LEGAL ISSUES IN STUDENT DISCIPLINE

What Is Due Process?

"Due process," as a Constitutional protection, is "an appropriate protection of the rights of an individual while determining his [or her] liability for wrongdoing and the
applicability of punishment" (Fisher 1970, p. 1). It is guaranteed by the Due Process Clause of the Constitution, which
requires that individuals must be afforded certain protections
before the government may deprive them of life, liberty, or
property. "For purposes of due process analysis, courts typically assume, without deciding, that a student has a property
interest in continued enrollment at a public institution"
(Kaplin and Lee 1995, p. 485). Since private colleges and
universities are not subject to Constitutional law, unless engaged in state action, they generally are not subject to these
requirements. The standard of due process used by the
courts in student conduct cases has been that of *fundamental fairness* (Ardaiolo 1983; Bakken 1968; Buchanan 1978;
Cole 1994; Fisher 1970; Footer, 1996; Kaplin and Lee 1995;
Young 1972).

Substantive due process refers to the purpose, nature, and
application of a rule or law. Applying the standard of fundamental fairness, rules must be clear and not overly broad,
they must have a fair and reasonable purpose, and they
must be applied in fairness and good faith.

Procedural due process relates to the rights of the accused
in the adjudication of an offense. That which is due, or ow-
ing, will vary depending on the seriousness of the offense
and on the severity of the possible sanction. Specifically, the
"Supreme Court has articulated a three-part test to resolve the
question of what process is due. Institutions must consider
the private interest at stake; the risk of an erroneous depriva-
tion of the private interest through the procedures used, and
the probable value, if any, of additional safeguards; and the
government's interest and the burdens that additional procedural requirements might entail (Footer 1996, pp. 24-25). The
balance courts seek is between the student's interest in not
being wrongly excluded versus the institution's interest in
maintaining discipline (*Goss v. Lopez* 1975).

Prior to the 1960s, under a combination of *in loco parentis* and contract theories, the courts generally assumed that
the college was acting fairly and in the best interest of the
student. However, during the civil rights movement, some
students were summarily dismissed from college for engag-

ing in civil rights demonstrations, which brought unprecedented legal scrutiny on procedural due process in disciplinary hearings, particularly dismissal proceedings (Bakken 1968). Since the landmark case of *Dixon v. Alabama State Board of Education* (1961) established that, in the instance of dismissal from a tax-supported college, due process requires that the student be given notice and a hearing, many court cases have recognized and extended the due process protections to student disciplinary proceedings that may result in the more serious sanctions such as suspension or expulsion. Although all of the procedural safeguards required in criminal proceedings are not required in student conduct hearings (Correnti 1988; Gehring and Bracewell 1992; Kaplin and Lee 1995; Pavela 1985; Shur 1983), and no one particular model of due process is expected (Bracewell 1988; Buchanan 1978; Travelstead 1987), the following basic procedural guidelines for serious cases, drawn from Pavela (1985), Footer (1996), and Kaplin and Lee (1995), are fairly well established:

- The most important principle of all, which applies equally to public and private institutions, is that the institution must follow its own rules, once established.
- A written statement (notice) of specific charges should be given to the student.
- The notice should include the names of witnesses and the nature of their proposed testimony. It should inform the student of the evidence the institution plans to use, and it should give the date, time, and location of the hearing.
- Once notified, the student should be given reasonable time to prepare a defense. The court requirements range from two to 10 days. "Providing at least three days notice of the date" is recommended by Footer (1996, p. 25).
- A hearing should be conducted wherein:
  —the student may bring an advisor;
  —the evidence against the student is presented;
  —the student may ask questions of witnesses, although not through counsel;
  —the student may present a defense, including their version of the facts, witnesses, and affidavits;
  —the accused student may be absent if he/she fails to appear, despite having been given reasonable written notice.

- The hearing may be "open" if the student has consented in keeping with the Family Educational Rights and Privacy Act.
- The determination of facts should be based solely on the evidence and testimony presented in the hearing.
- The student should be informed in writing of the decision, including the reasons, and the opportunity for appeal, if any, but no formal right of appeal is required.
- The hearing does not have to wait for the outcome of a criminal trial on the same facts.
- The role of legal counsel may be limited to consultation.
- The student may be asked questions, but refusal to answer may be the basis for negative inference (the student does not have a Fifth Amendment privilege against self-incrimination).
- A recording or transcription of the hearing should be made available to the student.

For more details, including suggestions about rules of evidence, burden of proof, composition of hearing panels, the role of attorneys, rules of evidence, and appeals, refer to Footer (1996, pp. 24-29) and Pavela (1985, pp. 42-45).

Concerns About "Proceduralism"

After the *Dixon* decision, most public, and many private, colleges and universities revised their disciplinary approach and established judicial processes that afforded much greater due process protection to students than before. Some went far beyond the *Dixon* requirements to include "full-blown adversarial hearings" (Pavela 1985, p. 41) and complex systems that looked and operated much like those of our criminal system. The result on some campuses was that the disciplinary process became "mired in legalistic disputes" (Lamont 1979, p. 85). This trend—often called "creeping legalism" or proceduralism—undermined the informal and uniquely educational element of college student discipline, it led to costly and time-consuming processes, and it placed the student and the institution in an unnecessarily adversarial relationship (Dannells 1977; Pavela 1985; Travelstead 1987). According to Travelstead (1987), there was much complaining and the courts were blamed, but "much of this complaining about excessive proceduralism and legalism is hollow. The excessive proceduralism, where it exists, has

... during the civil rights movement, some students were summarily dismissed from college for engaging in civil rights demonstrations, which brought unprecedented legal scrutiny on procedural due process ...

been largely caused by the institutions themselves" (p. 15). Pavela (1985) suggested that lack of proper legal advice and student pressure influenced the administrators who turned to the criminal system model, and he noted that "most schools now face a greater risk of being sued for running afoul of their own convoluted regulations . . . than for violating the simple standards of 'basic fairness' which the judiciary required" (p. 41).

Dannells' (1978, 1990) research indicated that the rush to create formal, criminal-like processes in disciplinary systems leveled off during the 1970s, and stabilized in the 1980s. In a comparison of data from surveys conducted in 1977 and 1987 on procedural due process, in four-year colleges and universities, few significant changes were found in the availability of due process mechanisms in dismissal cases. In terms of changes in substantive due process issues over the same period, Dannells (1990) found institutions became significantly more likely to publish their rules and procedures and to make them available by furnishing them to students, yet the frequency of student input into them had declined.

Academic Evaluation versus Student Misconduct
It is important to distinguish between academic evaluation and student misconduct because they have been treated differently in the courts. Codes of conduct typically proscribe both social and academic misconduct or dishonesty (cheating, plagiarism, etc.), and as Kaplin and Lee (1995) have noted, the courts have been relatively more deferential regarding the degree of protection required for students accused of academic misconduct. The courts have been even more deferential "when the evaluation of academic work is the issue, believing that such evaluation resides in the expertise of the faculty rather than the court" (p. 465).

The key case in due process and academic dismissal is *Horowitz v. Board of Curators of the University of Missouri* (1978). In it, the U.S. Supreme Court found that Horowitz, who had been dismissed from medical school for poor evaluations in clinical performance, patient and peer relations, and personal hygiene, was not entitled to a hearing. In essence, the court deferred to the faculty's judgment about her performance, and it seemed satisfied that she had received warning about her deficiencies and their consequences should they persist. As Kaplin and Lee (1995) have noted, because *Horowitz* involved clinical and interpersonal behavior, and was not a typical case of poor scholarship, it is a good example of the difficulty of categorization between that which is academic and that which is disciplinary, while demonstrating how hard it can be to distinguish between "fact-finding" in a disciplinary case versus "evaluation" or "academic judgment." That distinction may be even more blurred and problematic in cases where it is difficult to tell misconduct from poor scholarship, as sometimes occurs in alleged plagiarism (Travelstead 1987).

Courts do occasionally step in, as in cases where the academic evaluation has been arbitrary or capricious. That can be avoided by careful and conscientious deliberation of the "totality of a student's performance before deciding to dismiss for academic failure" (Cole 1994, p. 7).

Academic Misconduct
As stated earlier, the courts have been relatively deferential in cases involving academic misconduct, such as cheating and plagiarism, because they are more "academic" than "social." Nonetheless, such cases do entail fact-finding, and because their outcomes may be more stigmatizing and have more serious long-range consequences than purely academic judgments, Cole (1994) has recommended that public institutions should follow the same due process procedures in academic misconduct cases as they would in nonacademic hearings. Risacher and Slonaker (1996) have recommended that a model academic integrity policy should be based on four principles, one of which "is that academic penalties, i.e., grade penalties, should be separate from disciplinary penalties, e.g., suspension or dismissal" (p. 117). They seem to suggest "grade penalties" may be decided by faculty upon a unilateral determination of academic misconduct, while more serious penalties should be adjudicated through the campus disciplinary system. This kind of suggestion appears to confuse and blur the basic distinction between academic *misconduct* and academic *evaluation*, which seems problematic at best, and is not supported by the weight of expert opinion in the literature.

Once again, the public-private distinction operates here. "Private institutions may punish students for plagiarism without needing to decide if it is academic rather than nonacademic, as long as the institution's own rules regarding such are followed" (Cole 1994, p. 14). The standards of fundamental fairness and reasonableness, i.e., not arbitrary or capricious, apply in these cases as they do in matters of academic evaluation.

Sometimes institutions learn of academic misconduct after the student has earned the credit or degree, or the student misrepresents his/her academic record (e.g., transcript tampering) from the institution. In such cases, "both public and private colleges and universities have authority to revoke improperly awarded degrees [or credits] when good cause for doing so, such as discovery of fraud or misrepresentation, is shown" (Kaplin and Lee 1995, pp. 474-475; see also Cole 1994). Again, public institutions must provide the basic due process safeguards (notice and an opportunity to be heard), while private institutions must follow their rules in a fundamentally fair fashion and not act arbitrarily or capriciously.

The Issue of Group Behavior

The institution's educational authority and legal ability to discipline individual students is essentially unquestioned, but dealing with student groups and collective student behavior is more problematic. Much of the approach to college student discipline derives from the American tradition of individualism and the objective in our criminal system of protecting individual liberties, while adjudicating personal responsibility for wrong-doing. These principles, it could be argued, may be compromised through action by a college or university aimed at groups of students instead of each individual's behavior. Fraternal/social ("Greek") organizations, particularly men's fraternities, are often of concern in this regard. May an institution "discipline" a group of students without establishing, in a factual way, the misbehavior of each of its members? What legal issues surround this question?

It is well established in American case law that a college/university has the legal authority to sanction student groups whose collective behavior violates institutional rules that are in keeping with its mission, while not abridging the individual rights of students regarding free speech, association, and assembly (Kaplin and Lee 1995). Restrictions on student group activities, probation, and denial of institutional recognition have been challenged and upheld in courts in many states. In addition, statutes, such as the "anti-hazing" laws now in effect in at least 30 states (Gibbs 1992), provide the basis for criminal prosecution for some group activities.

Ultimately, the disciplinary leverage of the institution in dealing with student groups resides in its power to withhold or deny official recognition. In an effort to reduce institutional tort liability, some schools have instituted "recognition statements," which may, according to Kaplin and Lee (1995, p. 534), "limit the institution's authority to regulate the activities of the organization" while distancing it from the duty to supervise the group's activities. Institutions contemplating such statements should consider the recommendations:

1. *Description of the limited purpose of recognition.*
2. *Specification of the lack of principal-agent relationship between college and fraternity.*
3. *Acknowledgement that the fraternity is an independently chartered corporation existing under state laws.*
4. *Confirmation that the college assumes no responsibility for supervision, control, safety, security, or other services.*
5. *Restrictions on the use of the college's name, tax identification number, or other representations that the fraternity is affiliated with the college.*
6. *Requirement that the fraternity furnish evidence that it carries insurance sufficient to cover its risks* (Gulland and Powell 1989; cited in Kaplin and Lee 1995, p. 534).

Psychiatric Withdrawal of Disturbed Students
In recent years, college and university officials have reported that the number of emotionally disturbed students on campus has been increasing (Stuber and Dannells 1996). Gallagher, Harmon, and Lingenfelter (1994) found two-thirds of chief/senior student affairs officers reported an increase in the number of students with severe psychological problems on their campuses, and institutions have been reporting increased numbers of disruptions caused by emotionally disturbed students (Amada 1986; Tanner and Sewell 1979). The incidence of emotional disturbance in college students may be increasing at a rate higher than the general public, because many recently released psychiatric patients are now encouraged to go to college for purposes of personal development and recovery since nontraditional reentry students, who constitute the fastest growing segment of higher educa-

tion, seem to be at greater risk for mental and emotional problems (Dannells and Stuber 1992). Yet, there is evidence that on individual campuses, college officials tend to underestimate the actual rate of psychological problems in the student body (Stuber and Dannells 1996).

By federal law (both the Rehabilitation Act and the Americans with Disabilities Act), students may not be discriminated against (i.e., be legally withdrawn from school) on the basis of mental or psychological disabilities (Kaplin and Lee 1995). In some cases, disturbed students' behavior may disrupt the campus or pose a threat to the safety of themselves or others. Delworth (1989), in her Assessment-Intervention of Student Problems (AISP) model, made a useful distinction between students who are disturbing, those who are disturbed, and those who are both disturbed and disturbing. Those whose behaviors are disturbing, due to immaturity and/or selfishness, are properly channeled into the usual disciplinary process. Those who are disturbed, but who have not disrupted the campus environment, or broken any code of conduct rules, typically pose problems for themselves, but not others, and are referred to psychological services for assessment and treatment. It is the student who is both disturbed and disturbing, whose behavior is problematic *and* whose psychological state warrants assessment and perhaps treatment, who may be involuntarily withdrawn, pending a hearing wherein the usual due process safeguards are present (Pavela 1985).

Since the behavioral manifestations of a "protected" mental/medical condition may be dealt with through regular disciplinary processes, it is reasonable to question the wisdom of psychiatric withdrawal policies. Yet, as Brown and DeCoster (1989) noted, students in need of psychiatric care often do not see the relevance of such proceedings. Peer paraprofessionals and/or volunteers often staff these systems, and the campus community may need immediate protection. In short, normal channels may not be sufficient, in which case psychiatric withdrawal policies may be necessary.

Many colleges either do not have a clear policy for such cases (Dannells and Stuber 1992), or their policies give too much discretionary authority (Pavela 1985; Steele et al. 1984). After noting that 93 students were withdrawn from only seven institutions in two years, and one institution alone removed 21 during the same period, "some schools might be resorting to psychiatric withdrawals as an alternative to the traditional disciplinary process, by employing them to remove students who are simply perceived as troublesome or eccentric" (Steele et al. 1984, pp. 340-341).

"[M]any such students have the potential, with some degree of support, to complete college successfully. The immediate dismissal of these students at the first sign of difficulty raises considerable moral and legal questions" (Garland and Grace 1993, p. 73).

Campuses approaching policy formation in this area might do well to consider the Assessment-Intervention of Student Problems (AISP) model articulated in Delworth (1989). The AISP model makes clear and useful distinctions between disturbing students, disturbed students, and those who are both disturbing and disturbed, and it provides guidance about policy and procedure formulation for responding to behavioral and psychological problems of students. As Delworth and her colleagues point out, timely and accurate psychological assessment lies at the heart of any effective system of response to behavioral problems which might stem from mental illness or drug abuse.

The AISP model . . . provides guidance about policy and procedure formulation for responding to behavioral and psychological problems of students.

Confidentiality of Disciplinary Records

Several issues surround student disciplinary records (Wilson 1996), the most consistently problematic being their confidentiality and who has access to the information in them. In general, under the Family Educational Rights and Privacy Act (1974), also known as the Buckley Amendment or FERPA, disciplinary records are confidential and disclosures may be made to the student, to others only with the student's permission, or to others in the institution with a "legitimate" educational interest in the information. "Some campuses have interpreted this language to permit disclosures regarding the progress and outcome of disciplinary cases to complaining parties who are campus officials" (Wilson 1996, p. 48).

The confidentiality of student disciplinary processes, and resultant records, may be particularly problematic when students are included on hearing boards. FERPA does not expressly allow student board members access to records, so it may be a violation of it for student members of judicial panels to review prior conduct records in the course of deciding about sanctions or rehabilitative/educational responses. Furthermore, FERPA "would preclude holding an 'open' hearing without the consent of the accused student" (Pavela 1985, p. 43). It may be wise in all cases adjudicated before panels, which include student members for the institution, to secure the written consent of the accused student.

Open meeting laws (e.g., in Georgia; Wilson 1996) and campus crime reporting requirements are current issues related to student disciplinary records (Gehring 1995b) and FERPA, which reflect the law's continuing evolution in this area. In 1993, a Georgia court found that under the state's open meetings law, all hearings, including hearing panel deliberations, and their records were open to the public except in cases regarding academic dishonesty (Wilson 1996). As recently as January 1995, the U.S. Department of Education issued final rules amending FERPA to include disciplinary proceedings and subsequent actions. The law is still unclear with respect to records initiated by campus law enforcement officials, which might be subject to the Crime Awareness and Security Act of 1990 (Gehring 1995b). The Campus Security Act, as amended by the Sexual Assault Bill of Rights, requires that the accuser be informed as to the outcome of a disciplinary proceeding brought on an allegation of a sex offense. The accusers, in such cases, should be given written notice that the information is part of the accused's education record and may not be "redisclosed" without the signed written consent of the accused (Gehring 1995b).

The confidentiality of student disciplinary records, once presumably secure, is more complex and more at issue today than at any previous time. Campus administrators should be advised to consult with legal counsel regarding the management of those records and the evolving law affecting them.

Summary
Several, key legal issues surround the topic of student discipline: due process, academic evaluation versus misconduct, how to deal with group behavior, the psychiatric withdrawal of disturbed students, and the confidentiality of student disciplinary records. In each area, institutional leaders would be well served to maintain close and regular communication with legal counsel. *Fundamental fairness* is a reasonable and prudent rule-of-thumb and a worthy goal, not only in matters of due process, but in the other issues as well.

To the extent that an institution's policies are unclear (or perhaps nonexistent) in some of the areas, the risks of *ad hoc* policy formulation would seem too great. The chief student affairs officer would be the most logical leader to ensure that institutional policies in these areas are in keeping with current legal requirements. With respect to academic evaluation versus behavioral misconduct, the CSAO should certainly work in concert with the chief academic affairs officer in the process of policy formulation or clarification.

Once disciplinary policies and procedures are established, the institution must follow its own rules. This principle may seem obvious and simplistic, but its violation is a common point of court intervention.

STUDENT DISCIPLINE AND DEVELOPMENTAL THEORY

Seemingly in reaction to what many saw as the excessive proceduralism that followed the *Dixon* case, student affairs professionals in the last two to three decades have shown renewed interest in the educational nature of discipline and the application of human development concepts and theories to the conduct of disciplinary affairs. Not only is there concern for protection of the individual's rights, and of the institution itself, but there appears to be a growing realization of—or perhaps a return to—the primacy of the educational value in the disciplinary/judicial function. This is not to suggest that meeting students' legal rights and fostering their development are incompatible (Greenleaf 1978), but rather that the increasingly adversarial nature of the process has become a significant drain and distraction to those charged with administering their campuses' disciplinary system. It has become more difficult to find that proper balance necessary to the survival of the Student Personnel Point of View (Caruso 1978). However, with the growing body of theory, research, and literature on cognitive, moral, and ethical development, there appears to have been increasing interest in its application to the disciplinary setting (Saddlemire 1980).

Student discipline is, and always has been, an excellent opportunity for developmental efforts.

Student discipline is, and always has been, an excellent opportunity for developmental efforts. The traditional deans of students know this, of course, but they operated without the benefit of formal developmental theories, especially those that emphasize moral and ethical growth, which lend themselves to the disciplinary process. Much of discipline involves teaching (Ardaiolo 1983; Ostroth and Hill 1978; Travelstead 1987) and counseling (Foley 1947; Gometz and Parker 1968; Ostroth and Hill 1978; Stone and Lucas 1994; Williamson 1963; Williamson and Foley 1949). Through the application of developmental theory, the individual may be better understood, and counseling/developmental interventions may be more scientifically and accurately fashioned (Boots 1987).

Various developmental theories have been applied to the disciplinary process and its impact on the individual student (Boots 1987; Greenleaf 1978; Ostroth and Hill 1978; Smith 1978), and certain common elements and objectives of the different views and approaches are noted in the literature. First, insight is a commonly stated objective and a means to further growth in the individual "offender" (Dannells 1977). Second, self-understanding or clarification of personal identity, attitudes, and values, especially in relation to authority, for both the student, whose behavior is in question, and also for students who sit on judicial boards, is often described (Boots 1987; Greenleaf 1978). Third, the goals of self-control, responsibility, and accountability are often mentioned (Caruso 1978; Pavela 1985, 1992; Travelstead 1987). Fourth, the use of ethical dialogue, in both confronting the impact of the individual's behavior and its moral implications examining the fairness of rules, is receiving increased attention (McBee 1982; Pavela 1985; Smith 1978). Lastly, there appears to have been an extension of the scope and goals of student discipline, beyond that of simple adjudication and control/rehabilitation, to a broader objective of moral and ethical development as it relates to contemporary social issues, such as prejudice, health and wellness, sexism, racism, and human sexuality (Dalton and Healy 1984).

In a recent survey of college and university counseling center directors, Stone and Lucas (1994) found the following frequencies of goals for disciplinary counseling: assessment/evaluation, 28 percent; behavior change, 27 percent; student insight, 16 percent; education, 10 percent; establishment of appropriate goals, 5 percent; and "other," 14 percent. When asked to identify "reference material that the respondent would recommend for counseling center staff in working with disciplinary referrals" (p. 235), none of the counseling center directors offered developmental theory/theorists. This lack of reference to developmental theory may be taken as evidence of the oft-bemoaned theory-to-practice gap in the field of student affairs and may lend credence to the criticism of the usefulness of student development theory in our practice (Bloland, Stamatakos, and Rogers 1994).

Nonetheless, the weight of authority is clearly in keeping with an assertion that developmental theory can be a "proactive part of the total educational process" (Boots 1987, p. 67). It might be done this way:

> *For example, in working with a student involved in disruptive behavior and underage drinking at a residence hall party, the student affairs professional may render an informal assessment (King, 1990) of the student's level of moral reasoning at Level 1 (preconventional morality), Stage 2 (relative hedonism) using Kohlberg's (1969) model. Concurrently, using Chickering's (1969)*

theory, the student may be viewed as struggling with developing interpersonal competence and managing emotions. This may be a common diagnosis that would lend itself to a group intervention focusing on the campus regulations about alcohol, the reasons for them, and the ways that students can be socially engaged without using alcohol (Dannells 1991, p. 170).

Developmental theory is also useful for thinking about the relative maturity level of students (Thomas 1987) and about the positive outcomes for all students—not just "offenders"—involved in the disciplinary/judicial process.

Students may learn about community values and ethical principles when they either violate the conduct code or serve in judicial systems. The latter case represents an opportunity to develop integrity. In hearing cases, reviewing disciplinary procedures, and determining sanctions, students consider moral dilemmas in a concrete way. . . . By serving on hearing committees, students also benefit from watching faculty members, administrators, and staff members grapple with the arguments. The need for rules has not disappeared. . . . The challenge now is engaging students to take more responsibility for maintaining a safe and positive learning environment, becoming aware of the institution's code of conduct, and respecting the processes of enforcing and amending regulations (Chickering and Reisser 1993, p. 448).

The foregoing examples of the use and importance of developmental theory, in the context of disciplinary/judicial programs and interventions, are only introductory. A thorough overview of all the developmental theories and models, which are loosely called "student development theories," is well beyond the scope of this report. Excellent summaries of this body of knowledge are available in Knefelkamp, Widick, and Parker (1978), Moore (1990), Pascarella and Terenzini (1991), Rogers (1989), and Strange (1994).

Three theories or clusters of theories are seemingly most readily applicable to the disciplinary/judicial setting: the identity development theory of Chickering (1969) and Chickering and Reisser (1993); the moral development theories of Kohlberg (1969), Gilligan (1982), and Rest (1979);

and the intellectual and ethical development model of Perry (1970). The "involvement theory" of Astin (1985) is probably most useful in considering the general impact of disciplinary/judicial systems on the student volunteers and paraprofessionals who serve in them.

Here are 14 propositions that should be considered "for purposes of challenging practitioners and scholars to examine [the relevance of this body of knowledge] for what they practice and for how they come to inquire about and understand the college experience":

Who is the college student in developmental terms?

1. Students differ in age-related developmental tasks that offer important agendas for "teachable moments" in their lives.
2. Students differ in how they construct and interpret their experiences, and such differences offer important guides for structuring the education process.
3. Students differ in the styles with which they approach and resolve challenges of learning, growth and development, and such differences are important for understanding who and why students function in characteristic manners.
4. Students differ in the resolution of tasks of individuation according to their gender, culture-ethnicity, and sexual orientation; such differences offer important contexts for understanding the challenges students face in their search for personal identity.

How does development occur?

5. Development occurs as individuals reach points of readiness and respond to timely and appropriate learning experiences.
6. Development occurs as individuals respond to novel situations and tasks that challenge their current level or capacity.
7. Development occurs as individuals evaluate a learning task to be sufficiently challenging to warrant change and sufficiently supportive to risk an unknown result.
8. Development proceeds through qualitative and cyclical changes of increasing complexity.

9. Development occurs as an interactive and dynamic process between persons and their environments.

How does the college environment influence student development?

10. Educational environments restrict and enable individuals by the form and function of their natural and synthetic physical characteristics.
11. Educational environments exert a conforming influence through the collective, dominant characteristics of those who inhabit them.
12. Educational environments, as purposeful and goal directed settings, enable or restrict behavior by how they are organized.
13. The effects of educational environments are a function of how members perceive and evaluate them.

Toward what ends should development in college be directed?

14. Educational systems are embedded in various contexts of select values and assumptions that shape their expectations, processes, and outcomes (Strange 1994, pp. 402-409).

Those involved in developing and administering developmentally-oriented campus judicial systems would be well served to consider these propositions, particularly the last one, as it requires them to consider what the values are that provide direction for their institution, their program, and their interventions with individual students.

A Model for Bridging the "Theory-to-Practice Gap"

The so-called "theory-to-practice gap," which has been used to describe the difficulty of translating developmental theory to practice in student affairs work, is a very real concern in a field that is dominated by busy administrators and a body of knowledge and lexicon that does not readily lend itself to immediate application. Upcraft (1994) addressed this dilemma and recommended a "theory to practice to theory model" based on the work of Wells and Knefelkamp (unpublished manuscript), who developed an 11-step process based on the assumption that "educational goals are examined in the light of appropriate theory *before* interventions are designed and implemented." Those 11 steps, with some questions to apply them to disciplinary/judicial affairs, are:

1. *Identify pragmatic concerns.* What are the behavioral problems (e.g., alcohol abuse, sexual assault, academic dishonesty, vandalism) that need to be addressed?

2. *Determine educational goals and outcomes.* What behaviors, attitudes, values, etc., do you wish students to demonstrate or acquire?

3. *Examine which theories may be helpful.* What theories or clusters of theories are most related to the desired outcomes? Few, if any, practitioners are likely to take the time to study all of the many theories that could serve to illuminate their work; Pascarella and Terenzini (1991) estimated at least 20 identifiable theories useful for guiding policy and practice were advanced in the last two decades alone. Here, the suggestions in the foregoing section on entering this body of knowledge through one or more good summaries might be useful, or some consultation with a researcher/theoretician might help.

4. *Analyze student characteristics from the perspective of each theoretical cluster.* Which are most helpful in understanding these particular students?

5. *Analyze environmental characteristics from the perspective of each theoretical cluster.* On the basis of the student characteristics, what environmental characteristics are most salient in influencing them?

6. *Analyze the source of developmental challenge and support in the context of both student and environmental characteristics.* What are the specific challenges and supports for students? What is the proper balance for these students in this environment?

7. *Reanalyze educational goals and outcomes.* Are students ready for the intended outcomes? What objectives should be modified on the basis of the first six steps in this process?

8. *Design the learning process using methods that will facilitate mastery of the educational goals.* What sequence and structure of the disciplinary/judicial process is consistent with the goals of the program and the institu-

tion's mission? Elements to be considered include the process of involving students in the codification of the basic values of the community, how students are informed of the code of conduct and the process by which it is adjudicated, how students are trained in their roles in the process, how students are taught, counseled, sanctioned, etc., following a finding of a code violation.

9. *Implement the educational experience.* Programmatic implementation is the forte of most of the student affairs practitioners who are generally charged with this step.

10. *Evaluate the educational experience.* To what extent have the goals of the disciplinary/judicial program been met? What evidence is required to make judgments about the effectiveness of the program? Who needs to be satisfied with the results and by what standards will they judge them?

11. *Redesign the educational experience if necessary.* What changes are suggested by the foregoing step? How can the disciplinary system/program be improved based on the information and evaluation of its effectiveness? (Upcraft 1994, p. 439).

Implementing this model takes time and effort, and the questions posed are far simpler to ask than answer. Nonetheless, if disciplinary/judicial programs are to be more than mere mechanical applications of rules and sanctions, a careful and considered use of this, or a similar model, seems appropriate and necessary.

Summary
There exists a substantial body of developmental theory to guide the practice of student disciplinary affairs, but it can be hard for the practitioner to know where to start. Several good summaries of student development theory were suggested in the foregoing text, and a process model for bridging the "theory-to-practice gap" was offered.

THE SPECIAL ISSUE AND CHALLENGE OF DISCIPLINARY COUNSELING

As previously noted and defined, disciplinary counseling is one possible rehabilitative or educational response to student misconduct. It has a long history in the literature on student discipline (see ACE 1937, 1949; Gometz and Parker 1968; Snoxell 1960; Williamson 1956, 1963; Williamson and Foley 1949; Wrenn 1949), and it was a commonly accepted practice for most of this century. However, with the rise of professional mental health centers on campuses, administrators charged with the responsibility for discipline (along with many other duties) began sending students to counseling as a form of rehabilitation, often as a condition of continued enrollment, and often with the expectation that the counselor would make some report on the progress of the student's development, as insight about the student's future behavior. By definition, disciplinary counseling is mandatory, or nonvoluntary, unless one accepts the argument that the student can always choose dismissal rather than accept counseling, in which case it is, at least, coercive.

Referrals for disciplinary counseling appear to be on the increase, and disciplinary counseling is a widely practiced (Dannells 1990, 1991; Stone and Lucas 1994), despite being highly controversial on two counts: ethics and efficacy. Almost half (48 percent) of the counseling center directors surveyed by Stone and Lucas (1994) responded that counseling centers should not perform disciplinary counseling. The primary reservations given were ethics (involving issues of coercion, confidentiality, and role conflicts), management, and effectiveness issues. Stone and Lucas concluded that there is considerable confusion, ambivalence, and ambiguity about disciplinary counseling in the minds of counseling center directors. They called for a distinction between disciplinary *therapy* and disciplinary *education*, while at the same time admitting that such "sharply drawn conceptual differences often disappear in practice" (p. 238).

Not only is the hazy distinction between disciplinary counseling and disciplinary education problematic, "it is arguable whether an educational experience can be forced down the throat of an unwilling student with any more success than a psychotherapeutic experience can be forced down the throat of an unwilling client" (Gilbert and Sheiman 1995, p. 16).

Concluding that mandatory disciplinary psychotherapy for college students is unethical, Amada (1993), strenuously objected on several counts, noting that it:

... "it is arguable whether an educational experience can be forced down the throat of an unwilling student with any more success than a psychotherapeutic experience can be forced down the throat of an unwilling client ... "

*distorts and undermines the basis for corrective discipli-
nary action*

*often [is] motivated by fanciful and naive notions about
psychotherapy*

*unequivocally [is] a coercive measure that serves to instill
in the student resentment toward the therapist and therapy itself*

*lacks confidentiality [because some report to the referring
administrator is usually expected]*

*probably [is] in violation of the laws that protect persons
with handicaps from discriminatory treatment*

*tends to transfer the responsibility and authority for ad-
ministering discipline from where it rightly belongs—the
office of the designated administrator—to where it does
not belong—the offices of counselors and therapists* (pp.
128-130).

Gilbert and Sheiman (1995) echoed several of Amada's
concerns:

*Using mandatory psychotherapy as a form of disci-
pline in a university setting is a bad idea because it: (1)
is legally and ethically questionable; (2) doesn't work,
and it may hurt; (3) doesn't address behavior; (4)
damages the counseling center's integrity and effectiveness. On balance, the institution, the troubled student,
and the counseling center would be better off without
mandatory psychotherapy* (p. 6).

If disciplinary counseling should not be performed in counseling centers, should it be the duty of administrators who
also have the authority to sanction? If so, who is the "client"?
The student? The institution? Both? And if both, how does one
resolve a conflict between their needs? These, and the foregoing issues, are complex and challenging questions that deserve serious thought on the part of all who are engaged in
the design of campus judicial systems and who are involved
in the administration of the disciplinary process, especially as
it leads to prescriptions for mandatory counseling.

Summary
Disciplinary counseling is often required of students whose
behavior has been judged in violation of college rules, and it

is frequently noted in the literature as an appropriate reha-bilitative/educational response in disciplinary situations, but it has been challenged on the basis of ethics and effective-ness. At the very least, institutions that use it in their discipli-nary programs should clarify/define what it is, who does it, and to what end.

CONCLUSIONS AND RECOMMENDATIONS

[A] college or university is a *"disciplined"* community, a place where individuals accept their obligations to the group and where well-defined governance procedures guide behavior of the common good (*"Campus Life: In Search of Community,"* Carnegie Foundation for the Advancement of Teaching 1990, p. 37).

Conclusions

Student discipline was once a central part of the mission of American higher education; the colonial colleges aimed to shape the character of the leaders of their colonies and their churches. The many changes that have since reshaped our system of postsecondary education, particularly the university movement toward the continental model, moved student discipline to the periphery on most campuses. Faculty became much less involved, and student personnel specialists, and even judicial affairs specialists at larger schools, have effectively relieved the faculty and other administrators of responsibility for student conduct. With the demise of *in loco parentis* and the lowered age of majority, many colleges and most universities have been left without a philosophical compass to guide their approach to discipline. "The ambivalence college administrators feel about their overall responsibility for student behavior" (Carnegie Foundation 1990, p. 37), while disturbing, is perhaps not so surprising.

Present day concerns about such problems as crime on campus, hate speech, date/acquaintance rape, alcohol abuse, and academic dishonesty have been made public by an ever more scrutinizing press sensitive to demands for public accountability. College administrators are understandably wary of both demands for greater supervision of students and increasing litigiousness of civil liberty-minded students. Their preoccupation with judicial processes that mimic our criminal system, and ostensibly protect them and the institution from civil action, is likewise understandable.

Undergirding much of the controversy that continues to plague discipline is the lack of consensus over its meaning and purpose. Closely related is the issue concerning extent of jurisdiction, or the "reach," of the institution in student conduct. Several factors affect this issue, including the size, type, location, campus history and local tradition of the institution, but none more than the mission and the fundamental purpose that the college or university sets for itself. A smaller school with a more sharply focused mission will have a less complex task of defining or redefining its mission as it relates to student conduct. This task is most formidable at larger and state-supported universities that operate under omnibus mission statements.

We have a fairly clear, albeit general, picture of who is most "at risk" in disciplinary systems: The vast majority of the "offenders" on campus are the younger men, especially those who use or abuse alcohol. We also can anticipate that as the average age of our students continues to increase on most campuses, the origins of behavioral problems may shift from developmental issues of immaturity and impulsiveness to more deep-seated psychopathological difficulties. Assessment and intervention policies and strategies for alcohol-related and other mental health problems, which are sensitive to the constitutionally protected rights of students, are clearly necessary and in order.

Academic dishonesty is an old and common problem that has received considerable attention in recent years, for nothing cuts so deeply at the fabric of our most cherished educational values. Explicitly, we see a fundamental clash of cultures—faculty versus students—and the need to view and address problems at a cultural level is most apparent. The evidence is strong and convincing that colleges and universities need to combat the "cheating culture" with a broad-based, collaborative community strategy to promote the ethics of academic integrity and community responsibility.

Codes of conduct are the way institutions of higher education inform their students of their behavioral standards, the methods by which the rules are enforced and adjudicated, and the institution's response to violations. They must be specific enough to give adequate notice to students of behavioral expectations, while not so specific as to hamstring the school or challenge the students to find gaps in picky, excessively detailed lists of proscribed behaviors. Student input into the process of formulating the code, especially as it engages students in discussions about institutional and student values, is critical, yet it seems in recent years there has been a decline in student involvement in this way. The research on academic dishonesty, and the effectiveness of honor codes, strongly suggests that the code itself is not as important as the dialogue that is stimulated and reinforced by the process of its formulation and its regular review.

Hoekema's (1994) research on student codes of conduct led him to conclude that, after the decline of *in loco parentis* and the legal challenges of the 1960s and 1970s, most colleges' and universities' statements of behavioral standards became vacuous, and that they no longer clearly and effectively communicate institutional values. His work supported the Carnegie Foundation's assertion that "[i]n nonacademic matters, standards are ambiguous, at best" (Carnegie Foundation 1990, p. 37). He proposed an analytic framework and conceptual model for thinking about codes of conduct based on the three overarching moral/ethical principles of preventing harm, upholding freedom, and fostering community.

Research on the forms of organization and administration of disciplinary systems shows great diversity across institutions, considerable specialization at larger universities, and increasingly less involvement of the chief student affairs officer in discipline. Student involvement in hearing boards for the adjudication of code violations appears high. Campuses today employ a wide range of sanctions and educational responses to student misconduct, with alcohol education and disciplinary counseling on the increase.

In the years following the *Dixon* decision, colleges and universities rushed to institute procedural mechanisms for the protection of students' due process rights. Many went overboard and their infatuation with proceduralism and adversarialism led to rigidly criminalistic/legalistic judicial systems that bogged down the process and frustrated school officials and students alike. This trend has abated, yet many administrators have expressed the need for a return to simpler, less formal rules surrounding the hearing process.

In addition to the basic goal and necessity of maintaining an environment conducive to learning, student development, in some form (e.g., moral and ethical training, character formation, or education for citizenship), has been a fairly consistent objective of student discipline throughout the history of American higher education. The burgeoning growth of developmental theory, concurrent with our disenchantment with "legalism" over the last 20 or so years, has led to a new, or least renewed, interest in applying developmental theory to our work with students. Today's student affairs professionals, and their interested faculty colleagues, have an array of theories and models to frame their thinking and guide their formulation and evaluation of student devel-

Research on the forms of organization and administration of disciplinary systems shows great diversity across institutions.

opment programs, including student discipline. This body of knowledge is large and growing rapidly, so it is often difficult for those without formal training to know where to begin. Several good summaries and syntheses are now available as an entry into this subset of human development theory, and at least one application model is also available.

Disciplinary counseling is a commonly prescribed educational or rehabilitative response to student misconduct, but it presents a conundrum to both the administrators (or hearing boards), who request or require it and to the counselors who are asked to intervene and bring resolution. Administrators see it as a means of helping students develop insight and accept responsibility and the consequences for their behavior, while many counselors view mandatory/involuntary counseling as an ethical violation of their principle of respecting student/client autonomy. It has also been challenged on the grounds of efficacy; most counselors doubt the effectiveness of working with ostensibly recalcitrant clients who have not freely chosen to engage in counseling.

Recommendations

A community of learning, at its best, is guided by standards of student conduct that define acceptable behavior and integrate the academic and nonacademic dimensions of campus life. We found, however, that when it comes to regulations, students live in two separate worlds (Carnegie Foundation 1990, p. 37)

In these opening words to the chapter "A Disciplined Community" in *Campus Life*, we find the central theme of our recommendations:

> *the need to integrate the academic and nonacademic worlds of students through a broad-based, unified approach to student discipline that demonstrates and reinforces the importance and integrity of institutional values. The approach must be unified through the collaborative efforts of faculty, administrative staff, and students as they seek to ascertain just what those institutional values are, and how they can best be articulated and enforced for the good of the institution, and for the growth of the individual student.*

Colleges and universities should begin this process by

reviewing and clarifying institutional values as they are already articulated in mission statements, codes of conduct, and academic integrity policies. Perhaps the best and safest place to begin is with the latter because of the current high level of concern about student cheating, and because this area is ripe for collaboration between academic affairs and student affairs leaders. Academic affairs leaders, with input from their faculties, are in the best position to clarify the core values of the institution as they relate to academic integrity, while student affairs leaders are best positioned to communicate those values through orientation programs, as well as the publication and dissemination of key documents, such as the student handbook. Student affairs leaders are also well versed in the procedural requirements in the adjudication of misconduct.

> *Both [the National Association of Student Personnel Administrators'] "Reasonable Expectations" and [the American College Personnel Association's] "Student Learning Imperative" call for greater collaboration between student affairs and academic affairs to enhance student learning. One area in which this can take place is that of fostering academic integrity. There are many issues involved in breaches of academic integrity—institutional environments, expectations, rules and regulations, moral reasoning and legal rights and responsibilities* (Gehring 1995a, p. 6).

There are 12 "potential focal points for collaboration between academic affairs and student affairs." At least four of them fall directly within the area of student discipline or have direct implications for it. They are:

* *Manage disciplinary problems from a unified, rather than a unilateral, approach for consistency in response.*
* *Respond to alcohol and drugs on campus to prevent personal and academic debilitation.*
* *Respond to increased violence on campus.*
* *Respond to increased psychopathology, balancing the needs of troubled students and the community* (Garland and Grace 1993, p. 62).

Such broad initiatives will require, not only collaboration, but widespread community support as well.

There are 12 "potential focal points for collaboration between academic affairs and student affairs."

Hoekema's model is an excellent starting point for a college or university to use in reviewing its approach to matters of student conduct, because it requires that the institution first consider its existing goals in terms of basic moral ideals. His framework also provides a useful way of considering what behaviors are appropriate for disciplinary control. Campuses looking for a stimulus document for reviewing their disciplinary goals and code of conduct would be well served to consider Hoekema's book. It is not long, it is readable (and delightfully irreverent in places), and it was written by a scholar whose ideas may be more palatable to a skeptical faculty.

More campuses should seriously consider instituting an honor code. While they are certainly not a panacea, the very act of *considering* one would no doubt stimulate the kind of moral dialogue necessary for the campus to become a more moral community. This dialogue would certainly spill over into nonacademic conduct issues. The only possible drawback to stimulating this dialogue is dissension, which seems a reasonable sacrifice when the promise is so great.

The area of academic dishonesty, the idea of a "cheating culture" in the student body, and the need to foster peer support for academic integrity raise the importance of studying student behavior and how it is affected by the predominant student culture, the various student subcultures, and how it compares with the faculty culture. Besides conventional survey techniques to gather data about such things as levels of cheating, colleges and universities should consider qualitative methods in conducting "culture audits" (Kuh and Whitt 1988).

Institutional research should also be done on existing disciplinary programs to determine their present effectiveness. Like any other student development program, these efforts should be periodically and systematically evaluated to ensure that they are meeting their established goals. Those objectives should be defined in terms of measurable outcomes statements and evaluated on the basis of pre-established criteria and processes. It must be acknowledged that scientific research in this area has been, and will continue to be, difficult because of problems in identifying and controlling variables, in gathering data from program "participants," and in meeting the legal and ethical requirements for confidentiality and informed consent.

On a broader research front, student development theories need to be operationalized and tested in the disciplinary context. If traditional quantitative methods do not seem to convey the richness of data needed by disciplinary practitioners, then qualitative methods should be encouraged. The almost total lack of disciplinary case studies in the professional literature is surprising and should be remedied. Certainly, those who perform disciplinary functions on their campuses tell stories. Well written, detailed stories, that link problems to theory and interventions in thoughtful ways, would be an important contribution to the literature.

Colleges, universities, and their students would benefit by thinking about student discipline in less adversarial and more developmental ways. Many disputes that now fill campus judicial systems might be better resolved through mediation. If disciplinary counseling is too problematic in the way we currently think about our disciplinary/judicial systems, perhaps we need to reframe our approach to include such methods as "caring confrontation," wherein the student's behavior is critically examined in a supportive relationship, and the central goal of the process is to see what can be learned from the situation, and not so much the determination of guilt and the application of punishment.

Student affairs leaders, and in particular the chief student affairs officer (CSAO) on campus, must actively and positively embrace their responsibility to encourage the building of moral/ethical communities on campus. The best student discipline program is the preventative type that creates a campus environment of caring and compassion, and one that deters hateful and destructive behavior by virtue of commitment to the community. One of the most effective ways to achieve the building of such a commitment is through service learning. College students, especially young college students, who have had the opportunity to learn about the needs of others through service to them, are far less likely to engage in the kinds of selfish and immature behaviors that account for the bulk of the disciplinary caseloads at most institutions. CSAOs, with their expertise in experiential learning, and with the opportunity to promote such programs though a myriad of student services, are in a unique position to contribute to the curriculum in this way and to promote the development of the whole student, while helping themselves, and their student affairs colleagues "return to the academy" (Brown 1972).

Hoekema's model is an excellent starting point for a college or university to use in reviewing its approach to matters of student conduct, because it requires that the institution first consider its existing goals in terms of basic moral ideals.

The best and most central place to promote ethical campus communities and student development is in the curriculum (Levine 1992). Here is a recently-proposed "citizenship curriculum," which could foster the basic values undergirding the campus disciplinary program:

> *If we want our students to acquire the democratic virtues of honesty, empathy, generosity, teamwork, and social responsibility, we have to demonstrate those qualities not only in our individual professional conduct, but also in our institutional policies and practices. To emphasize the importance of these democratic virtues, why not begin a campus-wide effort to determine how citizenship and democracy can be given a more central place in the general-education curriculum?* (Alexander Astin 1995, p. B2).

Indeed, why not? Many colleges and universities are instituting interdisciplinary courses to meet general education needs and to challenge the values of a materialistic, aphilosophic student body. Might there not be a place for a course like "Individual Rights and Civic Responsibilities in the College and the Community?" Such an offering, possibly even a requirement, could be approached from several combinations of different disciplines, including political science, sociology, psychology, law, education, and philosophy/ethics. Faculty and student affairs professionals might team-teach the course, and the campus' primary disciplinary/judicial officer could play a central role in it as well. Course readings might include such diverse, yet relevant, books as *Habits of the Heart: Individualism and Commitment in American Life* (Bellah, Madsen, Sullivan, Swidler, and Tipton 1985), *College: The Undergraduate Experience in America* (Boyer 1987), *Campus Rules and Moral Community: In Place of In Loco Parentis* (Hoekema 1994), *Rights, Freedoms, and Responsibilities of Students* (Bryan and Mullendore 1992), *Coming of Age in New Jersey: College and American Culture* (Moffatt 1989), *The Age of Paradox* (Handy 1994), *The Spirit of Community: Rights Responsibilities, and the Communitarian Agenda* (Etzioni 1993), etc.

In a course like this, the subject of student conduct and moral/ethical development could be considered within the broader context of civic responsibility and community involvement. Students could be engaged in discussions on a range of topics that affect them as individuals on the campus, and that will continue to affect them as citizens beyond their college years. One such topic is the issue of hate speech codes, vis-a-vis freedom of speech and academic freedom. Students could be challenged to consider how the campus community can best balance protecting freedom of speech with its desire to protect those whose learning environment is negatively affected by speech that degrades or demeans them. The nature of prejudice and its occurrence in the human condition, and in society, could be explored through many lenses, including those of individual development and the development of campus culture. Another topic might be academic honesty, and how the institution should go about promoting it, and/or punishing those who violate it. Students could be educated in the values of the academy (e.g., the pursuit of truth) and taught the importance of appropriate and rigorous scholarly inquiry.

The teaching methods in a course of this nature should engage students "in active, social, cooperative modes of learning" (Gardiner 1994, p. 145), and it should provide its faculty with an opportunity to experience and model the power of cooperative methods. Students should be required to explore, reflect, and discuss, in a caring and supportive climate, that fosters not only their understanding, but ethical and emotional development as well. Thus, the moral dialogue inherent in a developmental approach to discipline (Pavela, 1985, 1996) could be brought to the classroom, with faculty and student affairs professionals collaborating for the benefit of their students and for the good of the campus community they share.

The importance of building new, more caring, and collaborative communities of learning on our campuses has been a consistent theme in the literature on higher education for almost a decade. Student discipline can play a vital part, but first institutions must clarify their values, and then campus leaders—including both academic affairs and student affairs—must take responsibility for developing judical programs which are fair, humane, and uphold those values for the betterment of the individual student and for the community as a whole.

APPENDIX A — MODEL STUDENT CODE

Article I: Definitions

1. The term [College] [University] means [name of institution].
2. The term "student" includes all persons taking courses at the [College] [University], both full-time and part-time, pursuing undergraduate, graduate, or professional studies and those who attend post-secondary educational institutions other than [name of institution] and who reside in [College] [University] residence halls. Persons who are not officially enrolled for a particular term but who have a continuing relationship with the [College] [University] are considered "students."
3. The term "faculty member" means any person hired by the [College] [University] to conduct classroom activities.
4. The term "[College] [University] official" includes any person employed by the [College] [University], performing assigned administrative or professional responsibilities.
5. The term "member of the [College] [University] community" includes any person who is a student, faculty member, [College] [University] official or any other person employed by the [College] [University]. A person's status in a particular situation shall be determined by [title of appropriate college or university administrator].
6. The term "[College] [University] premises" includes all land, buildings, facilities, and other property in the possession of or owned, used, or controlled by the [College] [University] (including adjacent streets and sidewalks).
7. The term "organization" means any number of persons who have complied with the formal requirements for [College] [University] [recognition/registration].
8. The term "judicial body" means any person or persons authorized by the [title of administrator identified in Article I, number 13] to determine whether a student has violated the Student Code and to recommend imposition of sanctions.
9. The term "Judicial Advisor" means a [College] [University] official authorized on a case-by-case basis by the [title of administrator identified in Article I, number 13] to impose sanctions upon students found to have violated the Student Code. The [title of administrator identified in Article I, number 13] may authorize a judicial advisor to serve simultaneously as a judicial advisor and the sole member or one of the members of a judicial body. Nothing shall prevent the [title of administrator identified in Article I, number 13] from authorizing the same judicial advisor to impose sanctions in all cases.
10. The term "Appellate Board" means any person or persons authorized by the [title of administrator identified in Article I, number 13] to consider an appeal from a judicial body's determination that a student has violated the Student Code or

from the sanctions imposed by the Judicial Advisor.

11. The term "shall" is used in the imperative sense.

12. The term "may" is used in the permissive sense.

13. The [title of appropriate administrator] is that person designated by the [College] [University] President to be responsible for the administration of the Student Code.

14. The term "policy" is defined as the written regulations of the [College] [University] as found in, but not limited to, the Student Code, Residence Life Handbook, and Graduate/Undergraduate Catalogs.

15. The term "cheating" includes, but is not limited to: (1) use of any unauthorized assistance in taking quizzes, tests, or examinations; (2) dependence upon the aid of sources beyond those authorized by the instructor in writing papers, preparing reports, solving problems, or carrying out other assignments; or (3) the acquisition, without permission, of tests or other academic material belonging to a member of the [College] [University] faculty or staff.

16. The term "plagiarism" includes, but is not limited to, the use, by paraphrase or direct quotation, of the published or unpublished work of another person without full and clear acknowledgment. It also includes the unacknowledged use of materials prepared by another person or agency engaged in the selling of term papers or other academic materials.

Article II: Judicial Authority

1. The Judicial Advisor shall determine the composition of judicial bodies and Appellate Boards and determine which judicial body, Judicial Advisor and Appellate Board shall be authorized to hear each case.

2. The Judicial Advisor shall develop policies for the administration of the judicial program and procedural rules for the conduct of hearings which are not inconsistent with provisions of the Student Code.

3. Decisions made by a judicial body and/or Judicial Advisor shall be final, pending the normal appeal process.

4. A judicial body may be designated as arbiter of disputes within the student community in cases which do not involve a violation of the Student Code. All parties must agree to arbitration, and to be bound by the decision with no right of appeal.

Article III: Proscribed Conduct

A. Jurisdiction of the [College] [University]

Generally, [College] [University] jurisdiction and discipline shall be limited to conduct which occurs on [College] [University] premises or which adversely affects the [College] [University] Community and/or the pursuit of its objectives.

B. Conduct—Rules and Regulations

Any student found to have committed the following misconduct is subject to the disciplinary sanctions outlined in Article IV:

1. Acts of dishonesty, including but not limited to the following:
   a. Cheating, plagiarism, or other forms of academic dishonesty.
   b. Furnishing false information to any [College] [University] official, faculty member or office.
   c. Forgery, alteration, or misuse of any [College] [University] document, record, or instrument of identification.
   d. Tampering with the election of any [College-] [University-] recognized student organization.
2. Disruption or obstruction of teaching, research, administration, disciplinary proceedings, other [College] [University] activities, including its public-service functions on or off campus, or other authorized non- [College] [University] activities, when the act occurs on [College] [University] premises.
3. Physical abuse, verbal abuse, threats, intimidation, harassment, coercion and/or other conduct which threatens or endangers the health or safety of any person.
4. Attempted or actual theft of and/or damage to property of the [College] [University] or property of a member of the [College] [University] community or other personal or public property.
5. Hazing, defined as an act which endangers the mental or physical health or safety of a student, or which destroys or removes public or private property, for the purpose of initiation, admission into, affiliation with, or as a condition for continued membership in, a group or organization.
6. Failure to comply with directions of [College] [University] officials or law enforcement officers acting in performance of their duties and/or failure to identify oneself to these persons when requested to do so.
7. Unauthorized possession, duplication or use of keys to any [College] [University] premises or unauthorized entry to or use of [College] [University] premises.
8. Violation of published [College] [University] policies, rules or regulations.
9. Violation of federal, state or local law on [College] [University] premises or at [College] [University] sponsored or supervised activities.
10. Use, possession or distribution of narcotic or other controlled substances except as expressly permitted by law.
11. Use, possession or distribution of alcoholic beverages except as expressly permitted by the law and [College] [University] regulations, or public intoxication.

12. Illegal or unauthorized possession of firearms, explosives, other weapons, or dangerous chemicals on [College] [University] premises.
13. Participation in a campus demonstration which disrupts the normal operations of the [College] [University] and infringes on the rights of other members of the [College] [University] community; leading or inciting others to disrupt scheduled and/or normal activities within any campus building or area; intentional obstruction which unreasonably interferes with freedom of movement, either pedestrian or vehicular, on campus.
14. Obstruction of the free flow of pedestrian or vehicular traffic on [College] [University] premises or at [College-] [University-] sponsored or supervised functions.
15. Conduct which is disorderly, lewd, or indecent; breach of peace; or aiding, abetting, or procuring another person to breach the peace on [College] [University] premises or at functions sponsored by, or participated in by, the [College] [University].
16. Theft or other abuse of computer time, including but not limited to:
    a. Unauthorized entry into a file, to use, read, or change the contents, or for any other purpose.
    b. Unauthorized transfer of a file.
    c. Unauthorized use of another individual's identification and password.
    d. Use of computing facilities to interfere with the work of another student, faculty member or [College] [University] Official.
    e. Use of computing facilities to send obscene or abusive messages.
    f. Use of computing facilities to interfere with normal operation of the [College] [University] computing system.
17. Abuse of the Judicial System, including but not limited to:
    a. Failure to obey the summons of a judicial body or [College] [University] official.
    b. Falsification, distortion, or misrepresentation of information before a judicial body.
    c. Disruption or interference with the orderly conduct of a judicial proceeding.
    d. Institution of a judicial proceeding knowingly without cause.
    e. Attempting to discourage an individual's proper participation in, or use of, the judicial system.
    f. Attempting to influence the impartiality of a member of a judicial body prior to, and/or during the course of, the judicial proceeding.

g. Harassment (verbal or physical) and/or intimidation of a member of a judicial body prior to, during, and/or after a judicial proceeding.

h. Failure to comply with the sanction(s) imposed under the Student Code.

i. Influencing or attempting to influence another person to commit an abuse of the judicial system.

C. Violation of Law and [College] [University] Discipline

1. If a student is charged only with an off-campus violation of federal, state or local laws, but not with any other violation of this Code, disciplinary action may be taken and sanctions imposed for grave misconduct which demonstrates flagrant disregard for the [College] [University] community. In such cases, no sanction may be imposed unless the student has been found guilty in a court of law or has declined to contest such charges, although not actually admitting guilt (e.g., "no contest" or "nolo contendere").

2. [Alternative A]
[College] [University] disciplinary proceedings may be instituted against a student charged with violation of a law which is also a violation of this Student Code, for example, if both violations result from the same factual situation, without regard to the pendency of civil litigation in court or criminal arrest and prosecution. Proceedings under this Student Code may be carried out prior to, simultaneously with, or following civil or criminal proceedings off-campus.
[Alternative B]
If a violation of law which also would be a violation of this Student Code is alleged, proceedings under this Student Code may go forward against an offender who has been subjected to civil prosecution only if the [College] [University] determines that its interest is clearly distinct from that of the community outside the [College] [University]. Ordinarily, the [College] [University] should not impose sanctions if public prosecution of a student is anticipated, or until law enforcement officials have disposed of the case.

3. When a student is charged by federal, state or local authorities with a violation of law, the [College] [University] will not request or agree to special consideration for that individual because of his or her status as a student. If the alleged offense is also the subject of a proceeding before a judicial body under the Student Code, however, the [College] [University] may advise off-campus authorities of the existence of the Student Code and of how such matters will be handled internally within the [College] [University] community. The [College] [University] will cooperate fully with law

enforcement and other agencies in the enforcement of criminal law on campus and in the conditions imposed by criminal courts for the rehabilitation of student violators. Individual students and faculty members, acting in their personal capacities, remain free to interact with governmental representatives as they deem appropriate.

Article IV: Judicial Policies

A. Charges and Hearings

1. Any member of the [College] [University] community may file charges against any student for misconduct. Charges shall be prepared in writing and directed to the Judicial Advisor responsible for the administration of the [College] [University] judicial system. Any charge should be submitted as soon as possible after the event takes place, preferably within [specified amount of time].

2. The Judicial Advisor may conduct an investigation to determine if the charges have merit and/or if they can be disposed of administratively by mutual consent of the parties involved on a basis acceptable to the Judicial Advisor. Such disposition shall be final and there shall be no subsequent proceedings. If the charges cannot be disposed of by mutual consent, the Judicial Advisor may later serve in the same matter as the judicial body or a member thereof.

3. All charges shall be presented to the accused student in written form. A time shall be set for a hearing, not less than five nor more than 15 calendar days after the student has been notified. Maximum time limits for scheduling of hearings may be extended at the discretion of the Judicial Advisor.

4. Hearings shall be conducted by a judicial body according to the following guidelines:
   a. Hearings normally shall be conducted in private. At the request of the accused student, and subject to the discretion of the chairperson, a representative of the student press may be admitted, but shall not have the privilege of participating in the hearing.
   b. Admission of any person to the hearing shall be at the discretion of the judicial body and/or its Judicial Advisor.
   c. In hearings involving more than one accused student, the chairperson of the judicial body, in his or her discretion, may permit the hearings concerning each student to be conducted separately.
   d. The complainant and the accused have the right to be assisted by any advisor they choose, at their own expense. The advisor may be an attorney. The complainant and/or the accused is responsible for pre-

senting his or her own case and, therefore, advisors are not permitted to speak or to participate directly in any hearing before a judicial body.

e. The complainant, the accused and the judicial body shall have the privilege of presenting witnesses, subject to the right of cross examination by the judicial body.

f. Pertinent records, exhibits and written statements may be accepted as evidence for consideration by a judicial body at the discretion of the chairperson.

g. All procedural questions are subject to the final decision of the chairperson of the judicial body.

h. After the hearing, the judicial body shall determine (by majority vote if the judicial body consists of more than one person) whether the student has violated each section of the Student Code which the student is charged with violating.

i. The judicial body's determination shall be made on the basis of whether it is more likely than not that the accused student violated the Student Code.

5. There shall be a single verbatim record, such as a tape recording, of all hearings before a judicial body. The record shall be the property of the [College] [University].

6. Except in the case of a student charged with failing to obey the summons of a judicial body or [College] [University] official, no student may be found to have violated the Student Code solely because the student failed to appear before a judicial body. In all cases, the evidence in support of the charges shall be presented and considered.

B. Sanctions

1. The following sanctions may be imposed upon any student found to have violated the Student Code:

a. Warning—A notice in writing to the student that the student is violating or has violated institutional regulations.

b. Probation—A written reprimand for violation of specified regulations. Probation is for a designated period of time and includes the probability of more severe disciplinary sanctions if the student is found to be violating any institutional regulation(s) during the probationary period.

c. Loss of Privileges—Denial of specified privileges for a designated period of time.

d. Fines—Previously established and published fines may be imposed.

e. Restitution—Compensation for loss, damage or injury. This may take the form of appropriate service and/or monetary or material replacement.

f. Discretionary Sanctions—Work assignments, service to the

[College] [University] or other related discretionary assignments (such assignments must have the prior approval of the Judicial Advisor).

g. Residence Hall Suspension—Separation of the student from the residence halls for a definite period of time, after which the student is eligible to return. Conditions for readmission may be specified.

h. Residence Hall Expulsion—Permanent separation of the student from the residence halls.

i. [College] [University] Suspension—Separation of the student from the [College] [University] for a definite period of time, after which the student is eligible to return. Conditions for readmission may be specified.

j. [College] [University] Expulsion—Permanent separation of the student from the [College] [University].

2. More than one of the sanctions listed above may be imposed for any single violation.

3. Other than [College] [University] expulsion, disciplinary sanctions shall not be made part of the student's permanent academic record, but shall become part of the student's confidential record. Upon graduation, the student's confidential record may be expunged of disciplinary actions other than residence-hall expulsion, [College] [University] suspension or [College] [University] expulsion, upon application to the Judicial Advisor. Cases involving the imposition of sanctions other than residence-hall expulsion, [College] [University] suspension or [College] [University] expulsion shall be expunged from the student's confidential record [insert preferred number] years after final disposition of the case.

4. The following sanctions may be imposed upon groups or organizations:

a. Those sanctions listed above in Section B.1., a through e.

b. Deactivation—Loss of all privileges, including [College] [University] recognition, for a specified period of time.

5. In each case in which a judicial body determines that a student has violated the Student Code, the sanction(s) shall be determined and imposed by the Judicial Advisor. In cases in which persons other than or in addition to the Judicial Advisor have been authorized to serve as the judicial body, the recommendation of all members of the judicial body shall be considered by the Judicial Advisor in determining and imposing sanctions. The Judicial Advisor is not limited to sanctions recommended by members of the judicial body. Following the hearing, the judicial body and the Judicial Advisor shall advise the accused in writing of its determination and of the sanction(s) imposed, if any.

C. Interim Suspension

In certain circumstances, the [title of administrator identified in Article I, number 13], or a designee, may impose a [College] [University] or residence-hall suspension prior to the hearing before a judicial body.

1. Interim suspension may be imposed only: a) to ensure the safety and well-being of members of the [College] [University] community or preservation of [College] [University] property; b) to ensure the student's own physical or emotional safety and well-being; or c) if the student poses a definite threat of disruption of or interference with the normal operations of the [College] [University].

2. During the interim suspension, students shall be denied access to the residence halls and/or to the campus (including classes) and/or all other [College] [University] activities or privileges for which the student might otherwise be eligible, as the [title of administrator identified in Article I, number 13] or the Judicial Advisor may determine to be appropriate.

D. Appeals

1. A decision reached by the judicial body or a sanction imposed by the Judicial Advisor may be appealed by accused students or complainants to an Appellate Board within five (5) school days of the decision. Such appeals shall be in writing and shall be delivered to the Judicial Advisor or his or her designee.

2. Except as required to explain the basis of new evidence, an appeal shall be limited to review of the verbatim record of the initial hearing and supporting documents for one or more of the following purposes:

   a. To determine whether the original hearing was conducted fairly in light of the charges and evidence presented, and in conformity with prescribed procedures giving the complaining party a reasonable opportunity to prepare and present evidence that the Student Code was violated, and giving the accused student a reasonable opportunity to prepare and to present a rebuttal of those allegations.

   b. To determine whether the decision reached regarding the accused student was based on substantial evidence, that is, whether the facts in the case were sufficient to establish that a violation of the Student Code occurred.

   c. To determine whether the sanction(s) imposed were appropriate for the violation of the Student Code which the student was found to have committed.

   d. To consider new evidence, sufficient to alter a decision, or other relevant facts not brought out in the original hearing, because such evidence and/or facts were not known to the person appealing at the time of the original hearing.

3. If an appeal is upheld by the Appellate Board, the matter shall be remanded to the original judicial body and Judicial Advisor for re-opening of the hearing to allow reconsideration of the original determination and/or sanction(s).

4. In cases involving appeals by students accused of violating the Student Code, review of the sanction by the Appellate Board may not result in more severe sanction(s) for the accused student. Instead, following an appeal, the [title of administrator identified in Article I, number 13] may, upon of the case, reduce, but not increase, the sanctions imposed by the Judicial Advisor.

5. In cases involving appeals by persons other than students accused of violating the Student Code, the [title of administrator identified in Article I, number 13] may, upon review of the case, reduce or increase the sanctions imposed by the Judicial Advisor or remand the case to the original judicial body and Judicial Advisor.

Article V: Interpretation and Revision

A. Any question of interpretation regarding the Student Code shall be referred to the [title of administrator identified in Article I, number 13] or his or her designee for final determination.

B. The Student Code shall be reviewed every [—] years under the direction of the Judicial Advisor.

APPENDIX B — STATEMENT OF ETHICAL PRINCIPLES AND STANDARDS OF CONDUCT

Preamble

The Association for Student Judicial Affairs (ASJA) is an organization of professional educators, many of whom hold responsibility for administering standards of student conduct within colleges and universities. The membership of ASJA believes that a primary purpose for the enforcement of such standards is to maintain and strengthen the ethical climate and to promote the academic integrity of our institutions. Clearly articulated and consistently administered standards of conduct form the basis for behavioral expectations within an academic community. The enforcement of such standards should be accomplished in a manner that protects the rights, health and safety of members of that community so that they may pursue their educational goals without undue interference.

As a means of supporting our individual commitments to fairness, honesty, equity and responsibility, the members of ASJA subscribe to the following ethical principles and standards of conduct in their professional practice. Acceptance of membership in ASJA signifies that the individual member agrees to adhere to the principles in this statement.

Use of This Statement

The purpose of this statement is to assist judicial affairs professionals in regulating their own behavior by providing them with standards commonly held by practitioners in the field. These standards may be useful in the daily practice of student judicial affairs work. Self-regulation is preferred. However, if a professional observes conduct that may be contrary to established principles, she/he is obligated to bring the matter to the attention of the person allegedly committing the breach of ethics. If unethical conduct continues, the matter may be referred to the offender's institution for appropriate action.

Ethical Principles and Standards of Conduct

Membership in ASJA implies agreement with and adherence to the following ethical principles and standards of conduct:

1. *Professional Responsibility.* Members have a responsibility to support both the general mission and goals of the employing institution and the rights, privileges and responsibilities of the students within that institution. Members shall make every

effort to balance the developmental and educational needs of students with the obligation of the institution to protect the safety and welfare of the academic community.

2. *Employment Obligations.* Acceptance of employment at an institution of higher education requires that members accept the general mission and goals of the institution and agree to adhere to the terms and conditions of the employment contract or letter of agreement for employment. Members shall adhere to the lawful tenets of the employee handbook or similar documents of the employing institution.

3. *Legal Authority.* Members respect and acknowledge all lawful authority. Members refrain from conduct involving dishonesty, fraud, deceit, misrepresentation or unlawful discrimination. ASJA recognizes that legal issues are often ambiguous and members should seek the advice of counsel as appropriate. Further, members shall demonstrate concern for the legal, social codes and moral expectations of the communities in which they live and work even when the dictates of one's conscience may require behavior as a private citizen which is not in keeping with these codes/expectations.

4. *Nondiscrimination.* Members shall conduct their professional duties and responsibilities in a manner that complies fully with applicable law and demonstrates equal consideration to individuals regardless of status or position. Members shall work to protect human rights and promote an appreciation of diversity and pluralism in higher education. Members do not engage in or tolerate harassment in any form nor do they enter into intimate relationships with those for whom they have any disciplinary, supervisory, evaluative, or instructional responsibility.

5. *Treatment of Students.* Members shall treat all students with impartiality and accept all students as individuals, each with rights and responsibilities, each with goals and needs; and seek to create and maintain a campus climate in which learning and personal growth and development take place. Further, members shall fully comply with the rules, regulations and procedural guidelines of the institution in enforcing its standards of conduct. Members shall not exceed their express authority in taking such actions.

6. *Development of Rules, Procedures and Standards.* Members shall strive to ensure that rules, procedures and standards for student conduct on their respective campuses meet legal requirements for substantive and procedural due process and reflect the general mission and goals of the institution. Further, they shall follow established procedures in making changes in such regulations. Finally, any such rules, procedures and standards shall reflect the commitment to equity, fairness, honesty, trustworthiness and responsibility.

7. *Student Behavior.* Members shall demonstrate and promote responsible behavior and seek to enhance the responsibility that each student takes for his/her own actions. Members support the principle of adherence to community standards and when those standards are violated, the necessity of disciplinary interventions that contribute to the educational and personal growth of the student. However, it is understood in situations where the behavior of a student poses a risk to self or others, members must take action consistent with applicable laws and the general mission and goals of the employing institution.

8. *Conflict of Interest.* Members shall seek to avoid private interests, obligations and transactions which are or appear to be in conflict of interest with the mission, goals, policies or regulations of their employing institution. Members shall clearly distinguish between those public and private statements and actions which represent their personal views and those which represent the views of their employing institution. Further, if members are unable to perform their duties and responsibilities in a fair and just manner due to prior involvement with a party or parties, they shall remove themselves from the decision-making process.

9. *Confidentiality.* Members ensure that confidentiality is maintained with respect to all privileged communications and to educational and professional records considered confidential. They inform all parties of the nature and/or limits of confidentiality. Members share information only in accordance with institutional policies and relevant statutes, when given informed consent, or when required to prevent personal harm to themselves or others.

10. *Accuracy of Information.* Members shall strive to assure that information provided for students, faculty, employees and employers, colleagues and the public is accurate and is accompanied by appropriate contextual material if needed.

11. *References.* Members shall provide only appropriate information regarding student conduct when providing references to potential employers, graduate schools or professional schools.

12. *Limitations.* Members are expected to understand the limits of their professional competencies and to refer students appropriately.

13. *Supervision.* Members who have supervisory responsibilities shall clearly define job responsibilities and regularly evaluate performance in accordance with institutional policies.

14. *Professional Responsibilities.* Members shall maintain and enhance professional effectiveness by improving skills and acquiring new knowledge, so that they may better serve both their students and their institutions. Further, members shall

seek to become active, involved members of their institutional communities and in professional associations and/or societies.

REVISED: *January 1993*
ASJA gratefully acknowledges the previous work on ethical principles and standards of conduct of the National Association of Student Personnel Administrators and the American College Personnel Association, as well as the work of numerous professionals throughout the country for their contributions toward the completion of this statement.

REFERENCES

Aaron, Ronald M. Winter 1992. "Student Academic Dishonesty: Are
Collegiate Institutions Addressing the Issue?" *NASPA Journal* 29:
107-113.

Amada, Gerald. April 1986. "Dealing With the Disruptive College
Student: Some Theoretical and Practical Considerations." *Journal
of American College Health* 34: 221-225.

———. 1993. "The Role of the Mental Health Consultant in Dealing
With Disruptive College Students." *Journal of College Student
Psychotherapy* 8: 121-137.

American College Personnel Association (ACPA), Commission on
Campus Judicial Affairs and Legal Issues. Summer 1993. *Model
Judicial Board Selection and Training Manual.* Washington, DC:
Author.

American Council on Education (ACE). 1937. *The Student Personnel
Point of View.* American Council on Education Studies, Series 1,
Vol. 1, No. 3. Washington, DC: Author.

———. 1949. *The Student Personnel Point of View.* Rev. ed.
American Council on Education Studies, Series 6, Vol. 13, No.
13. Washington, DC: Author.

Appleton, James R., Channing M. Briggs, and James J. Rhatigan.
1978. *Pieces of Eight.* Washington, DC: National Association of
Student Personnel Administrators.

Ardaiolo, Frank P. 1983. "What Process is Due?" In *Student Affairs
and the Law*, edited by Margaret J. Barr. New Directions for
Student Services No. 22. San Francisco: Jossey-Bass.

———, and Sally J. Walker. 1987. "Models of Practice." In
Enhancing Campus Judicial Systems, edited by Robert Caruso
and William W. Travelstead. New Directions for Student Services
No. 39. San Francisco: Jossey-Bass.

Association for Student Judicial Affairs (ASJA). 1993. *Statement of
Ethical Principles and Standards of Conduct.* Available on ASJA's
World Wide Web Homepage at <http://stulife.tamu.edu/asja/>.
College Station, TX: Author.

Astin, Alexander W. 1985. *Achieving Educational Excellence* San
Francisco: Jossey-Bass.

——— 1993. *What Matters in College?* San Francisco: Jossey-Bass.

———. October 6, 1995. "The Cause of Citizenship." *Chronicle of
Higher Education* B1.

Bakken, Clarence J. 1968. *The Legal Basis of College Student
Personnel Work.* Student Personnel Monograph Series No. 2.
Washington, DC: American Personnel and Guidance Association.

Barnett, David C., and Jon C. Dalton. November 1981. "Why College
Students Cheat." *Journal of College Student Personnel* 22: 545-551.

Bazik, A., and R. A. Meyering. 1965. "Characteristics of College Students Involved in Disciplinary Problems." *Journal of the National Association for Women Deans, Administrators, and Counselors* 28: 173-176.

Bellah, Robert N., William M. Sullivan, Ann Swidler, and Steven M. Tipton. 1985. *Habits of the Heart: Individualism and Commitment in American Life.* Berkeley, CA: University of California Press.

Bloland, Paul A., Louis C. Stamatakos, and Russell R. Rogers. 1994. *Reform in Student Affairs: A Critique of Student Development.* Greensboro, NC: ERIC Counseling and Student Services Clearinghouse, University of North Carolina. ED 366 862. 129 pp. MF-01; PC-06.

Boots, Cheryl C. 1987. "Human Development Theory Applied to Judicial Affairs Work." In *Enhancing Campus Judicial Systems*, edited by Robert Caruso and William W. Travelstead. New Directions for Student Services No. 39. San Francisco: Jossey-Bass.

Bowers, William J. 1964. *Student Dishonesty and Its Control in College.* New York: Columbia University Bureau of Applied Social Research.

Boyer, Ernest L. 1987. *College: The Undergraduate Experience in America.* New York, NY: Harper and Row.

Bracewell, William R. 1988. "Student Discipline." In *Student Services and the Law*, edited by Margaret J. Barr and Associates. San Francisco: Jossey-Bass.

Brady, Thomas A. 1965. "A University and Student Discipline." In *Student Discipline in Higher Education*, edited by Thomas A. Brady and Laverne F. Snoxell. Student Personnel Series No. 5. Washington, DC: American College Personnel Association.

Brown, Robert D. 1972. *Student Development in Tomorrow's Higher Education—A Return to the Academy.* Student Personnel Series No. 16. Washington, DC: American College Personnel Association. ED 067 975. 56 pp. MF-01; PC-02.

Brown, Virginia L., and David A. DeCoster. 1989. "The Disturbed and Disturbing Student." In *Dealing with the Behavioral and Psychological Problems of Students*, edited by Ursula Delworth. New Directions for Student Services No. 45. San Francisco: Jossey-Bass.

Brubacher, John S., and Willis Rudy. 1976. *Higher Education in Transition.* 3rd ed. New York: Harper and Row.

Bryan, William A., and Richard H. Mullendore, eds. Fall 1992. *Rights, Freedoms, and Responsibilities for Students.* New Directions for Student Services No. 59. San Francisco: Jossey-Bass.

Buchanan, E. T. "Joe," III. 1978. "Student Disciplinary Proceedings in Collegiate Institutions: Substantive and Procedural Due Process Requirements." In *The Legal Foundation of Student Personnel Services in Higher Education*, edited by E. H. Hammond and R. H. Shaffer. Washington, DC: American College Personnel Association.

Carnegie Foundation for the Advancement of Teaching. 1990. *Campus Life: In Search of Community*. Princeton, NJ: Author.

Carrington, Paul D. 1971. "On Civilizing University Discipline." In *Law and Discipline on Campus*, edited by Grace W. Holmes. Ann Arbor, MI: Institute for Continuing Legal Education.

Caruso, Robert G. 1978. "The Professional Approach to Student Discipline in the Years Ahead." In *The Legal Foundations of Student Personnel Services in Higher Education*, edited by E. H. Hammond and R. H. Shaffer. Washington, DC: American College Personnel Association.

Chickering, Arthur W. 1969. *Education and Identity*. San Francisco: Jossey-Bass.

————, and Linda Reisser. 1993. *Education and Identity*. 2nd ed. San Francisco: Jossey-Bass.

Cole, Elsa Kircher. 1994. *Selected Legal Issues Relating to Due Process and Liability in Higher Education*. Washington, DC: Council of Graduate Schools. ED 703 478. 45 pp. MF-01; PC-02.

Collison, Michele. January 17, 1990. "Apparent Rise in Students' Cheating Has College Officials Worried." *Chronicle of Higher Education*, A33.

Consolvo, Camille. February 1995. Unpublished report of the Association of Student Judicial Affairs' Substance Abuse Committee's Survey on Substance Abuse (C. Consolvo, Chair). Rolla, MO: University of Missouri-Rolla, Office of the Vice Chancellor for Student Affairs.

Correnti, Richard J. 1988. "How Public and Private Institutions Differ Under the Law." In *Student Services and the Law*, edited by Margaret J. Barr and Associates. San Francisco: Jossey-Bass.

Council for the Advancement of Standards for Student Services/Developmental Programs (CAS). 1988. *Standards and Guidelines for Judicial Programs and Services*. Washington, DC: Author.

Dalton, Jon C., and Margaret A. Healy. Fall 1984. "Using Values Education Activities to Confront Student Conduct Issues." *NASPA Journal* 22: 19-25.

Dannells, Michael. 1977. "Discipline." In *College Student Personnel Services*, edited by William T. Packwood. Springfield, IL: Thomas.

————. 1978. *Disciplinary Practices and Procedures in Baccalaureate-Granting Institutions of Higher Education in the United States.* Unpublished doctoral dissertation, University of Iowa, Iowa City, IA.

————. 1988. "Discipline." In *Student Affairs Functions in Higher Education,* edited by Audrey A. Rentz and Gerald L. Saddlemire. Springfield, IL: Thomas.

————. September 1990. "Changes in Disciplinary Policies and Practices Over 10 Years." *Journal of College Student Development* 31: 408-414.

————. March 1991. "Changes in Student Misconduct and Institutional Response Over 10 Years." *Journal of College Student Development* 32: 166-170.

————, and Donna Stuber. Spring 1992. "Mandatory Psychiatric Withdrawal of Severely Disturbed Students: A Study and Policy Recommendation." *NASPA Journal* 29: 163-168.

Delworth, Ursula. 1989. "The AISP Model: Assessment-Intervention of Student Problems." In *Dealing with the Behavioral and Psychological Problems of Students,* edited by Ursula Delworth. New Directions for Student Services No. 45. San Francisco: Jossey-Bass.

Dixon v. Alabama State Board of Education. 1961. 294 F. 2d 150.

Durst, Richard H. 1969. "The Impact of Court Decisions Rendered in the Dixon and Knight Cases on Student Disciplinary Procedures in Public Institutions of Higher Education in the United States." Doctoral dissertation, Purdue University, 1968. *Dissertation Abstracts* 29: 2473A-2474A. University Microfilms No. 69-2910.

Dutton, T. B., F. W. Smith, and T. Zarle. 1969. *Institutional Approaches to the Adjudication of Student Misconduct.* Washington, DC: National Association of Student Personnel Administrators.

Etzioni, Amitai. 1993. *The Spirit of Community: Rights, Responsibilities, and the Communitarian Agenda.* New York: Crown.

Family Educational Rights and Privacy Act of 1974, 20 U.S.C. § 1232g.

Fenske, Robert H. 1989. "Evolution of the Student Services' Profession." In *Student Services: A Handbook for the Profession,* 2nd ed., edited by Ursula Delworth, Gary R. Hanson and Associates. San Francisco: Jossey-Bass.

Fisher, Thomas C. 1970. *Due Process in the Student-Institutional Relationship.* Washington, DC: American Association of State Colleges and Universities. ED 041 189. 44 pp. MF-01; PC-02.

Fley, J. 1964. "Changing Approaches to Discipline in Student Personnel Work." *Journal of the National Association for Women Deans, Administrators, and Counselors* 27: 105-113.

Foley, John D. 1947. "Discipline: A Student Counseling Approach." *Educational and Psychological Measurement* 7: 569-582.

Footer, Nancy S. 1996. "Achieving Fundamental Fairness: The Code of Conduct." In *Critical Issues in Judicial Affairs: Current Trends in Practice*, edited by Wanda L. Mercer. New Directions for Student Services No. 73. San Francisco: Jossey-Bass.

Fowler, Gerald A. July 1984. "The Legal Relationship Between the American College Student and the College: An Historical Perspective and the Renewal of a Proposal." *Journal of Law and Education* 13: 401-416.

Frederickson, Jon. Winter 1992. "Disciplinary Sanctioning of Impulsive University Students." *NASPA Journal* 29: 143-148.

Gallagher, Robert P., William W. Harmon, and Christine O. Lingenfelter. Fall 1994. "CSAOs' Perceptions of the Changing Incidence of Problematic College Student Behavior." *NASPA Journal* 32: 37-45.

Gardiner, Lion.F. 1994. *Redesigning Higher Education: Producing Dramatic Gains in Student Learning.* ASHE-ERIC Higher Education Report No.7. Washington DC: The George Washington University, School of Education and Human Development.

Garland, Peter H., and Thomas W. Grace. 1993. *New Perspectives for Student Affairs Professionals: Evolving Realities, Responsibilities and Roles.* ASHE-ERIC Higher Education Report No. 7. Washington, DC: The George Washington University, School of Education and Human Development. ED 370 508. 152 pp. MF-0; PC-07.

Gehring, Donald D. April/May 1995a. "Abreast of the Law: Academic and Disciplinary Dismissals." *NASPA Forum* 15: 6.

———. November 1995b. "Abreast of the Law: New FERPA Amendments." *NASPA Forum* 16: 4.

———. February 1996. "Abreast of the Law: Alcohol and Sexual Abuse." *NASPA Forum* 16: 5.

———, and William R. Bracewell. 1992. "Standards of Behavior and Disciplinary Proceedings." In *Rights, Freedoms, and Responsibilities of Students*, edited by William A. Bryan and Richard H. Mullendore. New Directions for Student Services No. 59. San Francisco: Jossey-Bass.

———, and Gary Pavela. 1994. *Issues and Perspectives on Academic Integrity.* 2nd ed. Washington, DC: National Association of Student Personnel Administrators.

Genereux, Randy L., and Beverly A. McLeod. December 1995. "Circumstances Surrounding Cheating: A Questionnaire Study of College Students." *Research in Higher Education* 36: 687-704.

Gibbs, Annette. 1992. *Reconciling the Rights and Responsibilities of College Students: Offensive Speech, Assembly, Drug Testing, and Safety.* ASHE-ERIC Higher Education Report No. 5. Washington, DC: The George Washington University, School of Education and Human Development. ED 354 837. 108 pp. MF-01; PC-05.

Gilbert, Steven P., and Judith A. Sheiman. 1995. "Mandatory Counseling of University Students: An Oxymoron?" *Journal of College Student Psychotherapy* 9(4): 3-21.

Gilligan, Carol. 1982. *In a Different Voice.* Cambridge, MA: Harvard University Press.

Gometz, Lynn, and Clyde A. Parker. January 1968. "Disciplinary Counseling: A Contradiction?" *Personnel and Guidance Journal* 46: 437-443.

Gott v. Berea College. 1913. 156 Ky 376.

Goss v. Lopez. 1975. 419 U.S. 565.

Graham, Melody A., Jennifer Monday, Kimberly O'Brien, and Stacey Steffen. July 1994. "Cheating at Small Colleges: An Examination of Student and Faculty Attitudes and Behaviors." *Journal of College Student Development* 35: 255-260.

Greenleaf, Elizabeth A. 1978. "The Relationship of Legal Issues and Procedures to Student Development." In *The Legal Foundations of Student Personnel Services in Higher Education*, edited by Edward H. Hammond and Robert H. Shaffer. Washington, DC: American College Personnel Association.

Handy, Charles. 1994. *The Age of Paradox.* Cambridge MA: Harvard University Press.

Hanson, David J. January 27, 1995. "Student Alcohol Abuse Actually is on the Decline." Letter to the Editor. *Chronicle of Higher Education*, B5.

———, and Ruth C. Engs. Winter 1995. "Collegiate Drinking: Administrator Perceptions, Campus Policies, and Student Behaviors." *NASPA Journal* 32: 106-114.

Hayes, James A., and Cynthia P. Balogh. Spring 1990. "Mediation: An Emerging Form of Dispute Resolution on College Campuses." *NASPA Journal* 27: 236-240.

"High-tech Cheating." September 5, 1995. *National On-Campus Report* 23: 3.

Hodinko, Bernard A. June 1964. "A Study of Student Opinion Regarding Collegiate Discipline Situations." *Journal of College Student Personnel* 5: 217-219, 225.

Hoekema, David A. 1994. *Campus Rules and Moral Community: In place of In Loco Parentis*. Lanham, MD: Rowman & Littlefield.

Janosik, Steven M. 1995. "Judicial Decision-Making and Sanctioning: Agreement Among Students, Faculty, and Administrators." *NASPA Journal* 32: 138-144.

————, Mary B. Davis, and Edward F. D. Spencer. September 1985. "Characteristics of Repeat Student Offenders: A 6-Year Study." *Journal of College Student Personnel* 26: 410-414.

Jendrek, Margaret Platt. September 1989. "Faculty Reactions to Academic Dishonesty." *Journal of College Student Development* 30: 401-406.

————. May 1992. "Students' Reactions to Academic Dishonesty." *Journal of College Student Development* 33: 261-273.

Kaplin, William A., and Barbara A. Lee. 1995. *The Law of Higher Education*. 3rd ed. San Francisco: Jossey-Bass.

Kibler, William L. Summer 1993a. "Academic Dishonesty: A Student Development Dilemma." *NASPA Journal* 30: 252-264.

————. Fall 1993b. "A Framework for Addressing Academic Dishonesty from a Student Development Perspective." *NASPA Journal* 31: 8-18.

————. Winter 1994. "Addressing Academic Dishonesty: What Are Institutions of Higher Education Doing and Not Doing?" *NASPA Journal* 31: 92-101.

————, Sally Cole, Donald L. McCabe, Mary A. Olson, Gary Pavela, and Brenda Richardson. September 29, 1995. "Academic Integrity: The Truth of the Matter." A National Teleconference Addressing Issues of Academic Dishonesty (Donald Gehring, Coordinator). Bowling Green, OH: Bowling Green State University, Higher Education Doctoral Program and WBGV-TV.

————, Elizabeth M. Nuss, Brent G. Paterson, and Gary Pavela. 1988. *Academic Integrity and Student Development: Legal Issues and Policy Perspectives*. Asheville, NC: College Administration Publications.

King, Patricia M. 1990. "Assessing Development from a Cognitive-Developmental Perspective." In *College Student Development: Theory and Practice for the 1990s*, edited by Don G. Creamer and Associates. Alexandria, VA: American College Personnel Association.

Knefelkamp, Lee, Carole Widick, and Clyde A. Parker eds. 1978. *Applying New Developmental Findings*. New Directions for Student Services No. 4. San Francisco: Jossey-Bass.

Knock, Gary H. 1985. "Development of Student Services in Higher Education." In *Developing Effective Student Services Programs*,

edited by Margaret J. Barr, Lou A. Keating, and Associates. San
Francisco: Jossey-Bass.

Kohlberg, Lawrence. 1969. "Stage and Sequence: The Cognitive-
Developmental Approach to Socialization." In *Handbook of
Socialization Theory and Research*, edited by D. Goslin.
Chicago: Rand McNally.

Kuh, George D., and Elizabeth J. Whitt. 1988. *The Invisible Tapes-
try: Culture in American Colleges and Universities*. ASHE-ERIC
Higher Education Report No. 1. Washington, DC: The George
Washington University, School of Education and Human
Development.

Lamont, Lansing. 1979. *Campus Shock*. New York: Dutton. ED 299
934. 160 pp. MF-01; PC-07.

Lancaster, James M., Diane L. Cooper, and Ann E. Harman. Winter
1993. "Current Practices in Student Disciplinary Administration."
NASPA Journal 30: 108-119.

Lederman, Douglas. February 3, 1995. "Colleges Report Rise in
Violent Crime." *Chronicle of Higher Education* A31-32.

Lenning, Oscar T. January 1970. "Understanding the Student
Lawbreaker." *Journal of College Student Personnel* 11: 62-68.

Leonard, Eugenie A. 1956. *Origins of Personnel Services in
American Higher Education*. Minneapolis: University of
Minnesota Press.

Leslie, David W., and Ronald P. Satryb. September 1974. "Due
Process on Due Process: Some Observations." *Journal of College
Student Personnel* 15: 340-345.

Levine, Arthur E. April 10, 1992. "Changing Characteristics of Today's College Student." Chester E. Peters Lecture in Student
Development. Manhattan, KS: Kansas State University, College
of Education.

Ludeman, Roger B. March 1988. "A Survey of Academic Integrity
Practices in U.S. Higher Education." *Journal of College Student
Development* 29: 172-173.

May, Kathleen M., and Brenda H. Loyd. March 1993. "Academic
Dishonesty: The Honor System and Students' Attitudes." *Journal
of College Student Development* 34: 125-129.

McBee, Mary L. Summer 1982. "Moral Development: From Direction to Dialog." *NASPA Journal* 20: 30-35.

McCabe, Donald L., and William J. Bowers. January 1994. "Academic Dishonesty Among Males in College: A Thirty-Year
Perspective." *Journal of College Student Development* 35: 5-10.

———, and Gary Pavela. Spring 1993. "Academic Integrity: What
the Latest Research Shows." *Synthesis: Law and Policy in Higher*

Education 5: 340-343.

———, and Linda Klebe Trevino. September/October 1993. "Academic Dishonesty: Honor Codes and Other Contextual Influences." *Journal of Higher Education* 64: 522-538.

———, and Linda Klebe Trevino. January/February 1996. "What We Know About Cheating in College: Longitudinal Trends and Recent Developments." *Change* 28: 28-33.

Miller, Theodore K., and Judith S. Prince. 1976. *The Future of Student Affairs.* San Francisco: Jossey-Bass.

Moffatt, Michael. 1989. *Coming of Age in New Jersey: College and American Culture.* New Brunswick, NJ: Rutgers University Press.

Moore, Leila V., ed. Fall 1990. *Evolving Theoretical Perspectives on Students.* New Directions for Student Services No. 51. San Francisco: Jossey-Bass.

Ostroth, David D., Michael R. Armstrong, and Thomas J. Campbell, III. January 1978. "A Nationwide Survey of Judicial Systems in Large Institutions of Higher Education." *Journal of College Student Personnel* 19: 21-27.

———, and David E. Hill. Autumn 1978. "The Helping Relationship in Student Discipline." *NASPA Journal* 16: 33-39.

Pascarella, Ernest T., and Patrick T. Terenzini. 1991. *How College Affects Students.* San Francisco: Jossey-Bass.

Pavela, Gary. 1985. *The Dismissal of Students with Mental Disorders.* Asheville, NC: College Administration Publications.

———. July 29, 1992. "Today's College Students Need Both Freedom and Structure." *Chronicle of Higher Education,* B1-2.

———. Summer 1993. "A New Day for Honor Codes?" *Synthesis: Law and Policy in Higher Education* 5: 353-355.

———. 1996. "Judicial Affairs and the Future." In *Critical Issues in Judicial Affairs: Current Trends in Practice,* edited by Wanda L. Mercer. New Directions for Student Services No. 73. San Francisco: Jossey-Bass.

———, and Donald L. McCabe. Summer 1993. "The Surprising Return of Honor Codes." *Planning for Higher Education* 21: 27-32.

Perry, William G. 1970. *Forms of Intellectual and Ethical Development in College.* New York: Holt, Rinehart, & Winston.

Pezza, Paul E. March 1995. "College Campus Violence: The Nature of the Problem and Its Frequency." *Educational Psychology Review* 7: 93-103.

———, and Ann Bellotti. March 1995. "College Campus Violence: Origins, Impacts, and Responses." *Educational Psychology Review* 7: 105-123.

Phelps, Lisa, and Michael Burchell. No date. *A Guide to Creative Sanctions*. Washington, DC: American College Personnel Association, Commission on Campus Judicial Affairs and Legal Issues.

Ratliff, Richard C. 1972. *Constitutional Rights of College Students: A Study in Case Law*. Metuchen, NJ: Scarecrow Press.

Rest, James R. 1979. *Development in Judging Moral Issues*. Minneapolis: University of Minnesota Press.

Risacher, Joanne, and William Slonaker. Winter 1996. "Academic Misconduct: NASPA Institutional Members' Views and a Pragmatic Model Policy." *NASPA Journal* 33: 105-124.

Roffey, Arthur E., and David B. Porter. January 1992. "Moral Decision Making and Nontoleration of Honor Code Offenses." *Counseling and Values* 36: 135-149.

Rogers, Robert F. 1989. "Student Development." In *Student Services: A Handbook for the Profession*, edited by Ursula Delworth, Gary R. Hanson and Associates, 2nd ed. San Francisco: Jossey-Bass.

Roth, Nancy L., and Donald L. McCabe. November/December 1995. "Communication Strategies for Addressing Academic Dishonesty." *Journal of College Student Development* 36: 531-541.

Rudolph, Frederick. 1962. *The American College and University*. New York: Vintage Books.

Saddlemire, Gerald L. 1980. "Professional Developments." In *Student Services: A Handbook for the Profession*, edited by Ursula Delworth, Gary R. Hanson and Associates. San Francisco: Jossey-Bass.

Schetlin, E. M. 1967. "Disorders, Deans, and Discipline: A Record of Change." *Journal of the National Association for Women Deans, Administrators, and Counselors* 30: 169-173.

Seavey, Warren A. 1957. "Dismissal of Students: 'Due Process'." *Harvard Law Review* 70: 1406-1410.

Serr, Roger L., and Ralph S. Taber. 1987. "Mediation: A Judicial Affairs Alternative." In *Enhancing Campus Judicial Systems*, edited by Robert Caruso and William W. Travelstead. New Directions for Student Services No. 39. San Francisco: Jossey-Bass.

Seward, D. M. 1961. "Educational Discipline." *Journal of the National Association for Women Deans, Administrators, and Counselors* 24: 192-197.

Shea, Christopher. November 17, 1995. "A Sweeping Speech Code." *Chronicle of Higher Education*, A37.

Sherrill, Jan M., and Dorothy G. Seigel eds. 1989. *Responding to*

Violence on Campus. New Directions for Student Services No. 47. San Francisco: Jossey-Bass.

Shur, George M. 1983. "Contractual Relationships." In *Student Affairs and the Law,* edited by Margaret J. Barr. New Directions for Student Services No. 22. San Francisco: Jossey-Bass.

———. 1988. "Contractual Agreements: Defining Relationships Between Students and Institutions." In *Student Services and the Law,* edited by Margaret J. Barr and Associates. San Francisco: Jossey-Bass.

Sillers, Dan J., and Daniel D. Feder. March 1964. "Attitudes of General and Student Personnel Administrators Toward Student Disciplinary Problems." *Journal of College Student Personnel* 5: 130-140, 145.

Sims, O. S. 1971. "Student Conduct and Campus Law Enforcement: A Proposal." In *New Directions in Campus Law Enforcement,* edited by O. S. Sims. Athens, GA: University of Georgia, Center for Continuing Education.

Sisson, V. Shamin, and Sybil R. Todd. Summer 1995. "Using Mediation in Response to Sexual Assault on College and University Campuses." *NASPA Journal* 32: 262-269.

Sloan, John J. 1994. "The Correlates of Campus Crime: An Analysis of Reported Crimes On College and University Campuses." *Journal of Criminal Justice* 22(1): 51-61.

Smith, Alexander F. 1978. "Lawrence Kohlberg's Cognitive Stage Theory of the Development of Moral Judgment." In *Applying New Developmental Findings,* edited by Lee Knefelkamp, Carole Widick, and Clyde A. Parker. New Directions in Student Services No. 4. San Francisco: Jossey-Bass.

Smith, Daniel B. Winter 1994. "Student Discipline in American Colleges and Universities: An Historical Overview." *Educational Horizons* 72: 78-85.

Smith, George P., and Henry P. Kirk. April 1971. "Student Discipline in Transition." *NASPA Journal* 8: 276-282.

Smith, Michael Clay, and W. Richard Fossey. 1995. *Crime on Campus: Legal Issues and Campus Administration.* Phoenix, AZ: American Council on Education/Oryx Press Series on Higher Education.

Snoxell, Laverne F. December 1960. "Counseling Reluctant and Recalcitrant Students." *Journal of College Student Personnel* 2: 16-20.

———. 1965. "Due Process and Discipline." In *Student Discipline in Higher Education,* edited by Thomas A. Brady and Laverne F. Snoxell. Student Personnel Monograph Series No. 5.

Washington, DC: American Personnel and Guidance Association.

Steele, Brenton H., Deborah H. Johnson, and Scott T. Rickard. July 1984. "Managing the Judicial Function in Student Affairs." *Journal of College Student Personnel* 25: 337-342.

Stein, Ronald H. July 1972. "Discipline: On Campus, Downtown, or Both: A Need for a Standard." *NASPA Journal* 10: 41-47.

Stone, Gerald L., and Julie Lucas. January-February 1994. "Disciplinary Counseling in Higher Education: A Neglected Challenge." *Journal of Counseling and Development* 72: 234-238.

Stoner, Edward N., II, and Kathy L. Cerminara. Fall 1990. "Harnessing the 'Spirit of Insubordination': A Model Code of Disciplinary Conduct." *Journal of College and University Law* 17: 89-121.

Stuber, Donna, and Michael Dannells. [In Press]. "Responding to Behaviorally and Emotionally Disturbed Students: Assessment and Intervention Practices." *College Student Journal.*

Sutton, Michael E., and Mary E. Huba. Fall 1995. "Undergraduate Student Perceptions of Academic Dishonesty as a Function of Ethnicity and Religious Participation." *NASPA Journal* 33: 19-34.

Tanner, W. A., and J. D. Sewell. 1979. "The University Response Team: An Assessment. *Campus Law Enforcement Journal* 9: 28-31.

Thomas, Ryan. 1987. "Systems for Guiding College Student Behavior: Punishment or Growth." *NASPA Journal* 25: 54-61.

Tinto, Vincent. 1993. *Leaving College: Rethinking the Causes and Cures of Student Attrition.* Chicago: University of Chicago Press.

Tisdale, John R., and Frederick G. Brown. November 1965. "Characteristics of College Misconduct Cases." *Journal of College Student Personnel* 6: 359-366.

Tracey, Terence J., Margaret E. Foster, Douglas C. Perkins, and Lola P. Hillman. November 1979. "Characteristics of Student Offenders: Some New Findings and Suggested Improvements in Research Methodology." *Journal of College Student Personnel* 20: 492-497.

Travelstead, William W. 1987. "Introduction and Historical Context." In *Enhancing Campus Judicial Systems*, edited by Robert Caruso and William W. Travelstead. New Directions for Student Services No. 39. San Francisco: Jossey-Bass.

Upcraft, M. Lee. November 1994. "The Dilemmas of Translating Theory to Practice." *Journal of College Student Development* 35: 438-443.

Van Alstyne, W. W. 1963. "Procedural Due Process and State University Students." *UCLA Law Review* 10: 368-389.

Van Kuren, Nancy E., and Don G. Creamer. May 1989. "The Conceptualization and Testing of a Causal Model of College Student Disciplinary Status." *Journal of College Student Development* 30: 257-265.

Wechsler, Henry, Charles Deutsch, and George Dowdall. April 14, 1995. "Too Many Colleges Still in Denial About Alcohol Abuse." *Chronicle of Higher Education*, B1-2.

Williamson, Edmund G., W. Jorve, and B. Langarstedt-Knudsen. 1952. "What Kinds of College Students Become Disciplinary Cases?" *Educational and Psychological Measurement* 12: 608-619.

———. 1956. "Preventive Aspects of Disciplinary Counseling." *Educational and Psychological Measurement* 16: 68-81.

———. 1961. *Student Personnel Services in Colleges and Universities.* New York: McGraw-Hill.

———. January 1963. "A New Look at Discipline." *Journal of Secondary Education* 38: 10-14.

———, and John D. Foley. 1949. *Counseling and Discipline.* New York: McGraw-Hill.

Wilson, Jeanne M. 1996. "Processes for Resolving Student Disciplinary Matters." In *Critical Issues in Judicial Affairs: Current Trends in Practice*, edited by Wanda L. Mercer. New Directions for Student Services No. 73. San Francisco: Jossey-Bass.

Work, Gerald G. July 1969. "CPI Patterns of College Male Disciplinary Cases and a Comparison Group." *Journal of College Student Personnel* 10: 223-226.

Wrenn, C. Gilbert. 1949. "Student Discipline in College." *Educational and Psychological Measurement* 9: 625-633.

Young, Douglas P. 1972. "The Colleges and the Courts." In *The Yearbook of School Law 1972*, edited by L. J. Peterson and L. O. Garber. Topeka, KS: National Organization on Legal Problems of Education.

INDEX

A

academic dishonesty, 29

 competition and pressure for grades most important cause
of, 32

 effects of, 30

 factors affecting, 33-34

 student problem with definition of, 34

 what have institutions of higher education done to address,
36-37

 positively related to perception of peers' academic
dishonesty, 35

Academic Evaluation versus Student Misconduct, 70-71

academic honesty and how the institution should go about
 promoting   it as a topic of discussion, 99

Academic institutions

 have right to sanction student groups, 72, 72-73

 should follow same due process as in nonacademic
hearings, 71

Academic Misconduct, 71-72

administration of student discipline

 research on trends in, 60

administrators believe alcohol is increasingly involved in damage to
 campus property and violent behavior, 27

A Guide to Creative Sanctions, Phelps and Burchell, 65

AISP. *See* Assessment-Intervention of Student Problems model

alcohol. *See also* drinking

 abuse as a "moderate" to "major" campus problem

  two-thirds of college and university presidents rated, 27

 administrators believe is increasingly involved in damage to
   campus property and violent behavior, 27

 and Student Misconduct, 26-28

Amada (1993) concluded mandatory disciplinary psychotherapy is
 unethical, 87-88

American College Personnel Association, 63

 "Student Learning Imperative," 95

analyze environmental and student characteristics from the
 perspective of each theoretical cluster, 84

analyze the source of developmental challenge and support in the
 context of both student and environmental characteristics,
 84

Anderson and Gadaleto (1991)

 administrators believe alcohol is increasingly involved in
 damage

---

to campus property and violent behavior, 27

"anti-hazing" laws, 73

argument against disciplinary system based upon retributive
    punishment, 19

ASJA. See Association for Student Judicial Affairs

assessing student growth role of disciplinary specialist, 59

Assessment-Intervention of Student Problems model, 74, 75

Association for Student Judicial Affairs, 36, 61, 111

Astin (1985)

    Cooperative Institutional Research Program, 36

    "Involvement theory" of, 82

Authority to Discipline

    theories on, 19-22

B

Barnett and Dalton (1981)

    competition and pressure for good grades most important cause
        of
    academic dishonesty, 32

binge drinking, 27

bipartite system of discipline used on most campuses today, 11

"boxing" as a punishment at colonial colleges, 4

Boyer, Ernest

    disturbing ambivalence of college administrators with
        regard to
    responsibility for student behavior, 11

Brown and DeCoster (1989)

    students in need of psychiatric care do not see relevance of
    regular disciplinary processes, 74

Brubacher and Rudy (1976)

    Charles Eliot emphasis on three essential for university, 7

Buckley Amendment. See Family Educational Rights and Privacy
    Act

C

Cahn, Steven M., 51

Calvin College, 51

Calvinist doctrine

    influence on colonial colleges of, 3

campus alcohol policies

    questions on efficacy of, 27-28

campus disciplinary systems

    causes for variations in nature and scope, 57-58

Crime Awareness and Security Act of 1990, 76
criminalistic/legalistic judicial systems
   bogged down process, frustrated school officials and students,
      93
criminal system model
   lack of proper legal advice and student pressure caused
      administrators to turn to, 70
CSAO. See chief student affairs officer
"culture audits"
   should consider qualitative methods in conducting, 96
curriculum
         best and most central place to promote ethical campus
            communities and student development, 98

D
Dannells, Michael (Kansas State University professor), x
         campus officials more likely to refer violations of the law to
            civil authorities (1991), 23
         Disciplinary Hearing Boards commonly have both student
         and
         faculty and/or staff (1978, 1990), 62
   four-year colleges and universities had broadened the scope of
      their disciplinary authority (1990), 23
   research indicated that rush to create criminal-like processes
      leveled off and stabilized (1978, 1990), 70
dean of students office
   function in student discipline of, 58
Deans
         negative image of early, 9
         of Men/Women. See Deans of Students
         of Students origin, 8
"degradation" as a punishment at colonial colleges, 4
Delworth (1989)
   Assessment Intervention of Student Problems model, 74
"democratic humanization" movement, 7
design the learning process using methods that will facilitate
   mastery of the educational goals, 84-85
determine educational goals and outcomes, 84
developmental sanction. See environmental sanction
developmental terms
   who is the college student in, 82
developmental theories applied to the disciplinary process
         common elements and objectives of, 79-80

developmental theory

> can be a "proactive part of the total educational process," 80

> in college, 82-83

> new interest in applying to students, 93-94

> useful for thinking about the maturity level of students, 81

directive stance of institution toward

> undesirable behavior, 52

Disciplinary Affairs and Judicial Programs models, 60-61

disciplinary authority

> four-year colleges and universities had broadened the scope, 23

disciplinary case studies

> need to remedy absence in professional literature, 97

Disciplinary Counseling, 94

> as possible educational response to student misconduct, 87-89

> as the most used rehabilitative or reeducative action, 60

> role of disciplinary specialist in, 59

disciplinary education, 87

Disciplinary Hearing Boards, 61-63

> composition of, 62

disciplinary policies as primary source guiding how institutions address academic dishonesty, 36

Disciplinary Specialist basic functions, 58-59

disciplinary systems

> factors that cause variation in academe, 57

> have great diversity across institutions, 93

disciplinary therapy, 87

Discipline responsibility, 58

Dixon v. Alabama State Board of Education (1961), 60, 68

double jeopardy

> applies only to successive criminal proceedings, 22

drinking. *See also* alcohol *and* intoxication

> need to distinction between acceptable and unacceptable, 28

Due Process, 67-69

> at tax-supported college requires notice and a hearing, 68

> basic procedural guidelines for serious cases, 68-69

E

Educational Purpose theory determines Institutional Jurisdiction, 22

educational sanction. See environmental sanction

Eliot, Charles

Harvard president influential in defining Post Civil War Period, 7
emotionally disturbed students on campus
    increase in number of, 73
English residential college influence, 3
en loco parentis history, ix
environmentally-targeted responses to student misconduct, 64
environmental management role of disciplinary specialist, 59
environmental sanction, 63
Essentials for university according to Charles Eliot, 7
Ethical Principles and Standards of Conduct Statement
    Accuracy of Information, 113
    Confidentiality, 113
    Conflict of Interest, 113
    Development of Rules, 112
    Employment Obligations, 112
    Legal Authority, 112
    Limitations, 113
    Nondiscrimination, 112
    Professional Responsibilities, 111-112, 113-114
    purpose of, 111
    References, 113
    Student Behavior, 113
    Supervision, 113
    Treatment of Students, 112
evaluate the educational experience, 85
examine which theories may be helpful, 84

F
fabrication, 30
facilitating academic dishonesty, 30
faculty teaching and evaluation styles seem related to cheating, 34
Family Educational Rights and Privacy Act (1974), 75-76
FERPA. See Family Educational Rights and Privacy Act (1974)
"fighting words," 48
flogging as a punishment at Harvard, 4
Footer (1996)
    due process basic procedural guidelines for serious cases, 68-69
    framework for list of prohibited behaviors, 45
Fourteenth Amendment
    prevents public institutions of higher learning from engaging in
        activity that violates the federal constitution, 43
framework for list of prohibited behaviors, 45
Frederickson (1992)

flogging as a punishment at, 4

president influential in defining Post Civil War Period, 7

Hate Speech, 46-47

    problems, 46-49

    vis-a-vis freedom of speech as a topic of discussion, 99

High-tech Cheating, 32

historical rationale for student discipline, ix

Hodliko (1964) viewed as serious problems

    planning a demonstration and sexual promiscuity, 65

Hoekema (1994)

    administrators-only committees most common composition of
        Disciplinary Hearing Boards, 62

    found little emphasis on moral and social issues, except for
        academic dishonesty, in student handbooks, 46

    institution has effectively withdrawn from the field of morality
        and character formation, 24

    research revealed that codes of conduct have become
    vacuous, 93

    study of codes of conduct, 46

Hoekema's model of student discipline, 51-55

    excellent starting point for use in reviewing approach to
    maters

        of student conduct, 96

Honor Codes

    as an answer to academic dishonesty, 38-41

    as the best of many imperfect ways to promote and protect
        academic integrity, 41

    less cheating at schools with, 34

    need to consider implementation of, 96

    not prevalent as a source for guiding how institutions address
        academic dishonesty, 36

  Pavela (1993) list of advantages, 40-41

  Pavela (1993) list of disadvantages, 40, 40-41

  separate for other codes in three ways, 38-39

Horowitz v. Board of Curators of University of Missouri (1978), 70-71

I

identify pragmatic concerns, 84

identity development theory

  of Chickering (1996) and Chickering and Reisser (1993), 81

implement the educational experience, 85

"informative" disciplinary communications, 63

in loco parentis dealt apparently fatal blow, 10

Institutional Jurisdiction extent, 22-24
institutional response in a disciplinary situation
    factors that affect, 64-65
instruction role of disciplinary specialist, 59
intellectual and ethical development model
        of Perry (1970), 82
intoxication. See also drinking
        should not be accepted as an excuse for otherwise
        unacceptable
    behavior, 28
"Involvement theory" of Astin (1985), 82
"Issues in Academic Ethics," 51

J

Janosik (1995)
        findings consistent with Sillers and Feder (1964), 65
        most important information in judicial decision-making, 65
        planning a demonstration and sexual promiscuity not
        viewed as   serious problems, 65
Janosik, Davis, and Spencer (1985) study indicates possible to
        demographically describe most student disciplinary
        offenders, 25
Jendrek (1992) reporting of cheating by students, 33
judicial affairs specialists, 58
judicial tribunals. See Disciplinary Hearing Boards

K

Kansas State University professor. *See* Dannells, Michael
Kaplin and Lee (1995)
        courts more deferential regarding degree of protection
        required
            for students accused of academic misconduct, 70
        due process basic procedural guidelines for serious cases,
        68-69
        five major principles of free speech, 47
        Horowitz case involved clinical and interpersonal behavior
        and
            not typical case of poor scholarship, 71
        pointed out that courts rejected attempts by students in
        invoke
            self-incrimination, 22
        provide description of how custom relates to contract
        theory, 22

recognition statements limit rights of organization to regulate
   activities of groups, 73
Kibler (1993a) on cheating
   characteristics of student cheaters, 33
   faculty teaching and evaluation styles seem to be related to, 34
   frequencies of academic dishonesty, 31
Kibler (1994)
   what have institutions of higher education done to address
      academic dishonesty, 36-37
Kibler et al. (1995)
   recidivism in academic dishonesty on the rise, 31
Kohlberg (1969), Gilligan (1982) and Rest (1979)
   moral development theories of, 81

L

legalistic adversarial procedures adopted by many campuses, 11
legalistic or strict constructionist view of discipline, 19
Leonard (1956)
   decline in violence of student conduct in nineteenth century, 6
Ludeman (1988)
   need for institutional research to establish baseline data on
      academic dishonesty, 38

M

McCabe and Bowers (1994)
   percentage of students who admit to some form of cheating has
      been fairly stable, 31
McCabe and Pavela (1993)
   characteristics of student cheaters, 33
   less cheating at schools with honor codes, 34
      "repetitive test cheaters," 31
McCabe and Trevino (1993)
      frequencies of academic dishonesty, 31
      less cheating at schools with honor codes, 34
      study of influence of "contextual influences" on academic
         dishonesty, 35
mandatory disciplinary psychotherapy is unethical, 87-88
mandatory psychotherapy
      in a university setting as a form of discipline is a bad idea, 88
matters of procedure are likely to attract court intervention, 43
May and Loyd (1993)
      frequencies of academic dishonesty, 31
Miller and Prince (1976). See roles of the student discipline

nonoffenders more likely to have a parent or parents with a college degree, 25, 26

nonpathological origins of student misconduct, 26

nonregulatory approaches for dealing with hate speech should be emphasized, 47

"nontoleration" pledge, 39

O

open meeting laws, 76

organized student activities
    emergence of, 6

P

Pascarella and Terenzini (1991)
    at least 20 identifiable theories for guiding policy and practice advanced in last two decades, 84

Pavela (1985)
    due process basic procedural guidelines for serious cases, 68-69

lack of proper legal advice and student pressure caused administrators to turn to the criminal system model, 70
    rationale for the use of retributive punishment as a means for
    reaffirming personal responsibility, 19

Pavela (1992)
    Student Right-to-Know and Campus Security Act often require
    specific disciplinary policies, 17

Pavela (1993) list of honor codes disadvantages, 40, 40-41

Pavela and McCabe (1993)
    University of Maryland Code of Academic Integrity as a model, 37

pedagogical strategies that might lessen academic dishonesty, 37

peers' academic dishonesty
    academic dishonesty positively related to perceptions of, 35

People v. Wheaton College (1866), 20

permissive stance of institution toward undesirable behavior, 52

Perry (1970) intellectual and ethical development model, 82

personality characteristics of student offenders data old, fairly consistent and may not be subject to generational differences, 25

Personnel Movement in the Early 20th Century, 9

Phelps and Burchell *A Guide to Creative Sanctions,* 65

plagiarism, 30

planning a demonstration as a serious problem, 65

Post Civil War Period at colleges, 7-8

potential focal points for collaboration
between academic affairs and student affairs, 95

procedural due process, 67

"Proceduralism" concerns, 69-70

process
especially legal versus outcome (education) issue, 12
model for organizing & administering disciplinary function, 61
safeguards provision in administration of student discipline, 60
versus development issues, 12

program evaluation role of disciplinary specialist, 59

Psychiatric Withdrawal of Disturbed Students, 73-75
as an alternative to traditional disciplinary system, 74-75

psychopathology in college student seem to be on the rise, 26

psychotherapy
bad idea when mandatory in university setting as a form of discipline, 88

Public-Private dichotomy of academic institutions on codes of conduct, 43-44

public reprimands. *See* "degradation"

punitive sanction, 63

pure intellectualism view of discipline, 19

purpose of monograph in relation to student discipline, 1

purposes of Specific Areas of Discipline, 52

R

rationale for cheating, 32-33

reanalyze educational goals and outcomes, 84

"Reasonable Expectations" of
National Association of Student Personnel Administrators, 95

recidivism in academic dishonesty on the rise, 31

recognition statement policies for groups, 73

redesign the educational experience if necessary, 85

rehabilitative responses to student misconduct, 64

rehabilitative sanction, 63

"repetitive test cheaters," 31

reported increase of crime on campus, 14

reporting of cheating by students, 33

research on trends in administration of student discipline, 60

resident assistants
  violence against, 16
Rest (1979) moral development theories, 81
restrictive stance of institution toward undesirable behavior, 52
retaliatory abuse against those who make judicial complaints, 16
retributive punishment, 19
revisiting purpose of student discipline
  three new conditions requiring, ix
revoking of degrees, 72
Rights, Freedoms, and Responsibilities of Students, 98
Risacher and Slonaker (1996), 71
        confuse academic misconduct & academic evaluation
        distinction, 71
  model academic integrity policy principles, 71
roles of the student discipline specialist
  defined in terms of the basic student personnel functions, 59
Rutgers University
  conference on academic integrity at, 39

S

sanction should fit the offense rather the offender
  "crime and punishment" view of student discipline, 65
sanctions most commonly used, 63-64
self-incrimination
  courts rejected attempts by students to invoke, 22
service learning need, 97
severe psychological problems
  increase in number of students with, 15
sexual
        abuse is often alcohol related, 27
        Assault Bill of Rights, 76
        promiscuity as a serious problem, 65
"silent generation" of students, 9
Sillers and Feder (1964)
  Janosik (1995) findings consistent with, 65
Sloan (1994)
  steady increase in campus crime during 1985-1989, 14
Smith, Lynn
  computer networking as a resource for cheating, 32
Smith (1994)
  disciplinary systems today have process for enforcing
        regulations and distinct roles for individuals and
        committees, 57

U

undesirable behavior: directive, permissive & restrictive stance, 52
United States Air Force Academy, 39
universities that do not adequately inform students of their rules
    might be a basis for a student's defense or later legal appeal, 46
University of Manitoba, 32
University of Maryland Code of Academic Integrity, 37
University of Virginia
    first attempt to create honor code at, 38
Upcraft (1994) on "theory to practice to theory model", 83
USAFA
    See also United States Air Force Academy
U.S. Congressional 1990 Hearings on Campus Crime, 14

V

Van Kuren and Creamer (1989) state that
    little is known on origins of college disciplinary problems,
    25
    nonoffenders more likely to have a parent or parents with a
        college degree, 25
violations of the law
    campus officials more likely to refer to civil authorities, 23
violence against resident assistants, 16

W

Wells and Knefelkamp 11-step process, 83-85
what have institutions of higher education done to address
    academic dishonesty, 36-37
Why Do Students Cheat?, 32-36
Williamson (1963) definition of disciplinary counseling role, 59

Y

Yale University
    civil libertarian position, 48-9
"years of expansion", 6

ASHE-ERIC HIGHER EDUCATION REPORTS

Since 1983, the Association for the Study of Higher Education (ASHE) and the Educational Resources Information Center (ERIC) Clearinghouse on Higher Education, a sponsored project of the Graduate School of Education and Human Development at The George Washington University, have cosponsored the ASHE-ERIC Higher Education Report series. This series is the twenty-fifth overall and the eighth to be published by the Graduate School of Education and Human Development at The George Washington University.

Each monograph is the definitive analysis of a tough higher education problem, based on thorough research of pertinent literature and institutional experiences. Topics are identified by a national survey. Noted practitioners and scholars are then commissioned to write the reports, with experts providing critical reviews of each manuscript before publication.

Eight monographs (10 before 1985) in the ASHE-ERIC Higher Education Report series are published each year and are available on individual and subscription bases. To order, use the order form on the last page of this book.

Qualified persons interested in writing a monograph for the ASHE-ERIC Higher Education Report series are invited to submit a proposal to the National Advisory Board. As the preeminent literature review and issue analysis series in higher education, the Higher Education Reports are guaranteed wide dissemination and national exposure for accepted candidates. Execution of a monograph requires at least a minimal familiarity with the ERIC database, including *Resources in Education* and the current *Index to Journals in Education*. The objective of these reports is to bridge conventional wisdom with practical research. Prospective authors are strongly encouraged to call Dr. Fife at 800-773-3742.

For further information, write to
    ASHE-ERIC Higher Education Reports
    The George Washington University
    One Dupont Circle, Suite 630
    Washington, DC 20036
Or phone (202) 296-2597; toll free: 800-773-ERIC.

Write or call for a complete catalog.

Visit our web site at http://www.gwu.edu/~eriche

ADVISORY BOARD

James Earl Davis
University of Delaware at Newark

Cassie Freeman
Peabody College–Vanderbilt University

Susan Frost
Emory University

Mildred Garcia
Arizona State University West

James Hearn
University of Georgia

Philo Hutcheson
Georgia State University

CONSULTING EDITORS

Philip G. Altbach
State University of New York–Buffalo

Marilyn J. Amey
University of Kansas

Thomas A. Angelo
AAHE Assessment Forum

Louis C. Attinasi
Loyola University

Margaret J. Barr
Northwestern University

Robert Boice
State University of New York–Stony Brook

Robert A. Cornesky
Cornesky and Associates, Inc.

Barbara Gross Davis
University of California at Berkeley

James R. Davis
Center for Academic Quality and Assessment of Student
  Learning

Larry H. Ebbers
Iowa State University

Cheryl Falk
Yakima Valley Community College

L. Dee Fink
University of Oklahoma

Dean L. Hubbard
Northwest Missouri State University

Mardee Jenrette
Miami-Dade Community College

George D. Kuh
Indiana University

Robert Menges
Northwestern University

Diane E. Morrison
Centre for Curriculum and Professional Development

L. Jackson Newell
University of Utah

Sherry Sayles-Folks
Eastern Michigan University

Karl Schilling
Miami University

Pamela D. Sherer
The Center for Teaching Excellence

Lawrence A. Sherr
University of Kansas

Marilla D. Svinicki
University of Texas–Austin

David Sweet
OERI, U.S. Department of Education

Kathe Taylor
State of Washington Higher Education Coordinating Board

W. Allan Wright
Dalhousle University

Donald H. Wulff
University of Washington

Manta Yorke
Liverpool John Moores University

REVIEW PANEL

Charles Adams
University of Massachusetts–Amherst

Louis Albert
American Association for Higher Education

Richard Alfred
University of Michigan

Henry Lee Allen
University of Rochester

Philip G. Altbach
Boston College

Marilyn J. Amey
University of Kansas

Kristine L. Anderson
Florida Atlantic University

Karen D. Arnold
Boston College

Robert J. Barak
Iowa State Board of Regents

Alan Bayer
Virginia Polytechnic Institute and State University

John P. Bean
Indiana University–Bloomington

John M. Braxton
Peabody College, Vanderbilt University

Ellen M. Brier
Tennessee State University

Barbara E. Brittingham
The University of Rhode Island

Dennis Brown
University of Kansas

Peter McE. Buchanan
Council for Advancement and Support of Education

Patricia Carter
University of Michigan

John A. Centra
Syracuse University

Arthur W. Chickering
George Mason University

Darrel A. Clowes
Virginia Polytechnic Institute and State University

Cynthia S. Dickens
Mississippi State University

Deborah M. DiCroce
Piedmont Virginia Community College

Sarah M. Dinham
University of Arizona

Kenneth A. Feldman
State University of New York–Stony Brook

Dorothy E. Finnegan
The College of William & Mary

Mildred Garcia
Montclair State College

Rodolfo Z. Garcia
Commission on Institutions of Higher Education

Kenneth C. Green
University of Southern California

James Hearn
University of Georgia

Edward R. Hines
Illinois State University

Deborah Hunter
University of Vermont

Philo Hutcheson
Georgia State University

Bruce Anthony Jones
University of Pittsburgh

Elizabeth A. Jones
The Pennsylvania State University

Kathryn Kretschmer
University of Kansas

Marsha V. Krotseng
State College and University Systems of West Virginia

George D. Kuh
Indiana University–Bloomington

Daniel T. Layzell
University of Wisconsin System

Patrick G. Love
Kent State University

Cheryl D. Lovell
State Higher Education Executive Officers

Meredith Jane Ludwig
American Association of State Colleges and Universities

Dewayne Matthews
Western Interstate Commission for Higher Education

Mantha V. Mehallis
Florida Atlantic University

Toby Milton
Essex Community College

James R. Mingle
State Higher Education Executive Officers

John A. Muffo
Virginia Polytechnic Institute and State University

L. Jackson Newell
Deep Springs College

James C. Palmer
Illinois State University

Robert A. Rhoads
The Pennsylvania State University

G. Jeremiah Ryan
Harford Community College

Mary Ann Danowitz Sagaria
The Ohio State University

Daryl G. Smith
The Claremont Graduate School

William G. Tierney
University of Southern California

Susan B. Twombly
University of Kansas

Robert A. Walhaus
University of Illinois–Chicago

Harold Wechsler
University of Rochester

Elizabeth J. Whitt
University of Illinois–Chicago

Michael J. Worth
The George Washington University

RECENT TITLES

Volume 25 ASHE-ERIC Higher Education Reports

1. A Culture for Academic Excellence: Implementing the Quality Principles in Higher Education
   Jann Freed, Marie R. Klugman, and Jonathan D. Fife

Volume 24 ASHE-ERIC Higher Education Reports

1. Tenure, Promotion, and Reappointment: Legal and Administrative Implications (951)
   Benjamin Baez and John A. Centra

2. Taking Teaching Seriously: Meeting the Challenge of Instructional Improvement (952)
   Michael B. Paulsen and Kenneth A. Feldman

3. Empowering the Faculty: Mentoring Redirected and Renewed (953)
   Gaye Luna and Deborah L. Cullen

4. Enhancing Student Learning: Intellectual, Social, and Emotional Integration (954)
   Anne Goodsell Love and Patrick G. Love

5. Benchmarking in Higher Education: Adapting Best Practices to Improve Quality (955)
   Jeffrey W. Alstete

6. Models for Improving College Teaching: A Faculty Resource (956)
   Jon E. Travis

7. Experiential Learning in Higher Education: Linking Classroom and Community (957)
   Jeffrey A. Cantor

8. Successful Faculty Development and Evaluation: The Complete Teaching Portfolio (958)
   John P. Murray

Volume 23 ASHE-ERIC Higher Education Reports

1. The Advisory Committee Advantage: Creating an Effective Strategy for Programmatic Improvement (941)
   Lee Teitel

2. Collaborative Peer Review: The Role of Faculty in Improving College Teaching (942)
   Larry Keig and Michael D. Waggoner

3. Prices, Productivity, and Investment: Assessing Financial Strategies in Higher Education (943)
   Edward P. St. John

4. The Development Officer in Higher Education: Toward an Understanding of the Role (944)
   Michael J. Worth and James W. Asp II

Volume 21 ASHE-ERIC Higher Education Reports

Quantity   **Amount**

_____ Please begin my subscription to the current year's *ASHE-ERIC Higher Education Reports* (Volume 25) at $120.00, over 33% off the cover price, starting with Report 1.   _____

_____ Please send a complete set of Volume ___ *ASHE-ERIC Higher Education Reports* at $120.00, over 33% off the cover price.   _____

Individual reports are available for $24.00 and include the cost of shipping and handling.

SHIPPING POLICY:

- Books are sent UPS Ground or equivalent. For faster delivery, call for charges.
- Alaska, Hawaii, U.S. Territories and Foreign Countries, please call for shipping information.
- Order will be shipped within 24 hours after receipt of request.
- Orders of 10 or more books, call for shipping information.

All prices shown are subject to change.

Returns: No cash refunds—credit will be applied to future orders.

PLEASE SEND ME THE FOLLOWING REPORTS:

Quantity	Volume/No.	Title	Amount

Please check one of the following:
☐ Check enclosed, payable to GWU-ERIC.
☐ Purchase order attached.
☐ Charge my credit card indicated below:
    ☐ Visa   ☐ MasterCard

Subtotal: _____

Less Discount: _____

Total Due: _____

Expiration Date_____

Name_____

Title_____

Institution _____

Address_____

City _____ State _____ Zip_____

Phone _____ Fax _____Telex_____

Signature _____ Date_____

SEND ALL ORDERS TO: ASHE-ERIC Higher Education Reports
The George Washington University
One Dupont Cir., Ste. 630, Washington, DC 20036-1183
Phone: (202) 296-2597 • Toll-free: 800-773-ERIC
FAX: (202) 452-1844
http://www.gwu.edu/~eriche